THE BOY WHO SAW TRUE

THE BOY
WHO SAW TRUE

With an

Introduction, Afterword and Notes

by

CYRIL SCOTT

THE C. W. DANIEL COMPANY LTD
1 Church Path, Saffron Walden
Essex CB10 1JP, United Kingdom

First Published 1953

Reprinted 1961
Second impression, August 1966
Third impression, September 1969
Fourth impression, July 1971
Fifth impression, November 1974
Sixth impression, September 1978
Seventh impression, August 1982
Eighth impression, July 1986
Ninth impression, August 1988
Tenth impression, June 1991
Eleventh impression, September 1994
Twelfth impression, June 1998
Thirteenth impression, August 2001

© SL 1953
ISBN 0 85435 493 X

Production in association with
Book Production Consultants plc,
25–27 High Street, Chesterton,
Cambridge CB4 1ND

Printed in England by the Bath Press

CONTENTS

INTRODUCTION

D URING the course of my twofold career as a musical composer and a writer on occult and other matters, I have from time to time received manuscripts from various persons (mostly women) who were optimistic enough to imagine that a preface from my pen would give added weight to their literary efforts! Some of them have even asked me to give out that they (the authors) were reincarnations of various eminent personages! This of course I declined to do, for the nature of their scripts was in itself enough to prove that such assertions were simply the outcome of vanity. As to scripts dealing with communications with the disembodied and clairvoyance in general, these may be interesting to those persons who still want to be convinced as regards personal survival, but there is a sameness about them which is apt to become tedious to the already convinced.

The Boy Who Saw True, however, comes into a totally different category, and differs materially from all the hundreds of books I have read on Spiritualism and kindred subjects. In fact not one of them displayed the characteristics of this highly diverting human document,

7

with its naive candours, its drolleries, its unconscious humour, its oscillations between the ridiculous and the exalted, and perhaps I may venture to add, its power to convince for the very reason that the young diarist never set out with the intention of carrying conviction. Here was a precocious young boy who was born with a talent for clairvoyance (as some children are born with a talent for music) and who could see auras and spirits, yet failed to realise that other people were not similarly gifted. In consequence he was misunderstood and had to suffer many indignities. But apart from all this, the document is of interest in that it reveals the thoughts, emotions and perplexities of a Victorian youngster brought up a little prior to the "naughty nineties": though for my own part I think it a pity that he insisted on deleting so much of the diary and only retaining those parts which he thought would be amusing or instructive to the public. This has even given rise to the suggestion that I had been hoaxed over the manuscript; though the many friends to whom I lent the typescript violently repudiated such an idea. In view of such conflicting opinions, I can only say this; namely that during the course of my life I have known at least thirty people—some of them intimately—who possessed to varying degrees that extension of vision manifested by the young diarist. Further, I believe that the day is not far hence when many children will be born with the same faculties that he possessed and may be equally misunderstood. Besides which "fellow feeling makes us wondrous kind," and I remember my own childhood and its perplexities and emotions. Incidentally it is of astrological interest to note that we both had the same sun-sign, Sun in Libra at birth which may account for certain characteristics we possessed in common, though obviously he had a different rising sign to account for his remarkable psychic faculties.

The following details supplied by the diarist's widow should now be stated. Before his death his wife persuaded him to let the diary be published. But he made certain stipulations. It was not to be printed till several years after his death, and some of the names were to be altered, as he did not wish to cause any embarrassment to surviving relatives and acquaintances. (It says much for his sense of humour that where any of the real names had a somewhat comic ring, he amused himself by substituting others of a similar comicality.) Further, he insisted on improving the punctuation in Part I, and " doctoring " a number of passages where the bad spelling and grammar would merely irritate rather than amuse the reader. However, in other cases he allowed bad spellings to remain, and where these occur no unjust aspersions should be cast on printers and proof readers. As to the title, he refused to let any more high-sounding one be used than the name this book now bears; nor was the author's identity to be mentioned. His wife suggested that someone who had written books on occult subjects should be induced to write an introduction. To this he had no objection, but modestly imagined that no such writer would be found!

With regard to the diarist himself: he was born in the North of England, his father being a business man, but with a taste for reading. His son seems to have inherited this taste, and already when quite young had literary aspirations, which account for some of the comicalities to be found in the script. He would steal into his father's library and read books which, as his mother remarked when taking them away from him, were "not at all suitable for little boys." And doubtless she was quite right; though as it so happens the results of the precocious lad's "naughtiness" have proved highly diverting in the end . . . at least so I have found.

At the conclusion of the diary I have added more extensive details about the diarist's life.

CYRIL SCOTT

Eastbourne, December, 1952.

PART I

THE DIARY

Note : The comments in brackets were made by the diarist when preparing the script for publication.—C.S.

1885

Jan. 1.

Arnold, my best chum, said he was going to keep a dairy in the new year, and so I said I would keep one too, and hoped it'ud get printed some day like the dairy in pa's shelf by Mr. Pepys. When I told Mildred (my elder sister) she bet me a pennorth of assydrops I'd get tired of it in a week. But when I told pa and ma, pa said, " That's right, my lad, you keep a dairy. Though always remember this—a thing worth doing at all is worth doing well. So mind you write it nicely, and when you don't know how to spell a word, ask somebody who does." And ma said, " Yes;

and mind you don't forget what your father says." So I had to say I wouldn't, though I did feel rather provoked, because I can never do anything without ma or pa wanting to give me a lecture . . . Mildred is in the dumps because we have just been told that we have to start lessons again on Tuesday, and Mildred says it is beastly unfair of pa not to let us have as long holidays as the schools. But pa says he doesn't hold with these long holidays, and that when children have nothing to do, they only get into mischief. Mildred says pa is a horrid old slave driver. How vexed he would be if he knew . . . I can't think of anything more to say.

Jan. 2.

Pa got up on the wrong side of the bed this morning and complained of his liver, and was nasty with ma, and said his bacon was too salt and his egg hard boiled and all. And I felt very uncomfy and thought it wasn't fair, because it was Susan's fault and not ma's, and pa had no bizzness to say such things. Pa was very vexed too, because the cat made a smell in the house, and pa said if we couldn't teach our pets better manners, we oughtn't to have any. Then Mildred got sourcy and said it wasn't our fault if the cat got diorear. So ma made her learn a collect off by heart for being rood to her father. I do wish Mildred wouldn't take liberties with pa like that. I always know when pa has liver because his lights are all dirty, and she must know too. But it is no use talking to Mildred, she only tells me to hold my noise. (The meaning of this cryptic reference to " lights " becomes apparent anon.)

Ma says on Sundays I am only to put down about sacred things in my dairy, things about church and all that. But that I can stick down the other things by heart next day if I like. After church to-day, I asked what to commit adultry means. Pa sort of looked up at the ceiling and said, What next! and ma went red and said, " don't ask so many questions," and Janet made a rood noise and left the room post haste, and we could hear her bursting outside the door. Then Mildred and I giggled because she had made that rood noise, and ma frowned and told us to behave ourselves. But when I asked Mildred afterwards why this thusness, she said she didn't know. I thought it very funny, I must say! because committing adultry comes in the commandments, and the curate reads them out in church.

Ma took me to the dentist this afternoon to have my tooth stopped with some stuff like silver paper. I asked him if he liked being a dentist and fiddling inside people's mouths, and he said he didn't much mind. Then I said, " But it must be a bit nasty for you if people have been eating onions." And he laughed a bit and said, " Yes, it was not so pleasant then." And ma giggled a bit too, but looked as if she thought I oughtn't to have passed this remark, because only common people eat onions. When we got home, I thought for a joke I would like to play at being a dentist too, and make some pocket money. So I took some silver paper out of an old chocolate box and

13

made it into little pills to stop people's teeth with, and then put them in a bottle. Then I told Susan (the cook) that when she had tooth-ake, I would stop her tooth for tuppence. But afterwards Mildred, who said I was a softie, told me Susan had false teeth which didn't have to be stopped, and I felt disappointed . . . .

Jan. 8.

I told Mildred to-day that I had won my bet and that she must give me the assydrops, because I hadn't got tired of my diary (correctly spelt this time) in a week as she said I would. But she answered she'd only give me them if I showed her what I'd put down. So I said, that wasn't fair, and that it was private. Then she snatched the book from me and began to read it, and laughed and said, " Why, you don't even know how to spell the thing." (I had omitted to correct the spelling in the previous entries.) What will you pay me to milk the cows? " You go and milk yourself," I said in a wax. (Evidently, I was quite unaware of the significance of this ribald retort.) " Don't be rood," she cried. " And if you want to know, d-i-a-r-y spells diary, and d-a-i-r-y spells buttermilk. Sucks for you." Then she pulled snooks at me and threw my nice copy-book at my face. I wish I was four years older than her instead of the other way about, I'd soon give her "what for," I would *that* . . . . Ma looked poorly to-day, and sighed at dinner, and said, like she often does, " I wish we could do without eating." So do I when there is cold mutton and horrid rice pudding or that awful blammonge. Before our afternoon lessons I made friends again with Mildred, and said I'd let her

14

off the assydrops if she'd promise not to read my diary again. And she promised. But I'm going to hide it all the same, to be on the safe side.

Jan. 16.

To-day we began lessons again with scriptures. I am always glad when it is about Jesus and not about Jehovah, because I think Jehovah is a horrid old gentleman, but I love Jesus. This morning it was all about Jesus's circumcision, which I have just looked up in the bible because I forgot how it spelt. Of course we had to ask Miss Griffin what a circumcision was, but she said she couldn't be sure, but thought they cut a bit of skin out of a baby's forehead (spelt forred) and that it made a mark. So Mildred said, it must have hurt like billyo, and asked if they gave the baby cloroform; and Miss Griffin got a bit tight, and said, no. (This libellous aspersion on Miss Griffin's character was my primitive way of indicating that she drew herself up and became rigid). After that I thought I'd ask her about adultry, as ma wouldn't tell me, but she only blushed and said we'd understand when we were grown up, and then she blew her nose. " Well, you might at least tell us this much," said Mildred; " Have *you* ever committed adultry?" " Good gracious! dear, of course not," said she, and got as red as a turkey cock. " Then I think you *might* tell us what it means,' said Mildred, " 'cause if you won't, I shall look it up in the dic." " I forbid you to do any such thing," said Miss Griffin. " If you *must* know I would rather tell you myself. When a man is so wicked that he wants to marry some one who is married already, that's called committing adultry." " Oh, is that

15

all," said Mildred, " then why didn't you tell us before?'
" You didn't mind telling us about Cain and Abel the
other day," said I, "and it'ud be much wickeder if I
killed Mildred, than if I wanted to marry Antie Maude
who's married to Uncle John." "No one ever marries
their Antie," said Miss Griffin, getting quite tight. Miss
Griffin always gets tight when she's vexed. (Poor
repressed spinster, without a grain of humour! Her
attempts to get out of the predicament in which we had
involved her were only to lead to a worse one in the
end). When Miss Griffin had gone, Mildred was very
disobedient and went straight to the dic. to look for
adultry, but she didn't know what any of the words
meant, neither did I . . . .

Jan. 18.

I asked ma at breakfast for a box with a key I had
seen in the toy-shop for my next birthday present.
When ma wanted to know what for, I said, to lock up
my diary in. Then she laughed a bit, but said, very well,
I could have it if I was a good boy . . . . This afternoon
was ma's at home, and about fifty old ladies called (a
gross exaggeration) and made an awful noise in the
drawing-room like the tower of Babel. In the middle of
it, ma came out into the hall with a very red face,
because she always gets red when there are a lot of
people, and shouted to us to come down and say how do
you do to old Mrs. Bennett. (Not that my mother ever
shouted, she called melodiously). Then after we had
done this to Mrs. Bennett and all the rest of them, and
I had felt very uncomfy, ma said, " Well, now you can
run along." And that was the end of that. Afterwards

when ma came up into the nursery, I asked her who was the old party with eyebrows like pa's moustash: and she said, "Wherever did you pick that up?" So I told her that Hobbs (the gardener) always called people that, and she said it was very rood, and I wasn't to let her hear me say it again. But I shall jolly well say it in my diary if I want to, because I don't see why I should'nt.

Jan. 20.

To-day we went to the dancing class, and I have fallen in love again. She is called Florrie, and she has a sweet face and soft blue eyes, and Mildred says she is 16. I wish I could see her cry. I shan't mind going to bed so much to-night, then I can think of her and pretend she is crying and I am hugging her and telling her not to cry . . . . (From about the age of four I was constantly falling in love with girls very much older than myself, and I always pictured them in distress and my diminutive self acting the part of comforter. Sometimes I fell in love solely as the result of seeing a girl or young woman in tears. Tender sentiments, however, were never aroused in me by little girls of my own age).

Jan. 22.

As it is Mildred's birthday, papa and mama gave her a game for sundays called the Pilgrim's Progress, and I gave her a shilling box of paints which mama paid for. Mamma said that now we are so big she wants us to give over saying pa and ma, and that we are to call our parents mother and father or mamma or papa, because only common people or very little children say ma and pa . . . . We are let off our lessons to-day, and this

17

afternoon Arnold and Ethel and Henry are asked to tea and to play games. Mother can't come because she has to sell things at a Sale of Work, but Susan and Janet are to be allowed to play with us in the nursery, and Mrs. Prettyman, who father always calls old Mrs. Stick-in-the-mud, is coming to answer the front door bell.

Jan. 30.

Mr. Wilcox called to-day and came up to the nursery and brought me a lovely train that goes on lines. I love Mr. Wilcox, we have such fun when he comes, and he plays the piano to me, and I like that better than anything, and want to be an organist when I grow up. Mamma has asked him to dinner on sunday because his cook is ill in bed, and there is no body to cook his sunday dinner properly, so I expect we shall have fowl and bread-source, and he will like to have his little joke. (I should mention that the Rev. Stanley Wilcox was the Curate in Charge of the church my parents frequented.) I told Mr. Wilcox that I was keeping a diary, and he said that he kept one himself, and when anything struck him he put it down. He said he didn't write his diary every day, because it was silly to put down things like I got up, I had bacon for breakfast, I went to bed, I washed my hands and all the rest of it. And so I said, I thought it was silly too, because what was the use. And he looked quite pleased and said, "I'm so glad you agree with me." I suppose it was naughty, but I didn't tell him I *had* put down some of these silly things; but I have just crossed them out, and so that will make it all right. Tommy made a smell again to-day, and when papa got in, I heard him say,

" Pooh! this is beyond a joke, we shall have to get rid of that cat." I feel awful, because if pussy is sent away my heart will break, like Mrs. Buddle told mamma hers did when Mr. Buddle died.

Feb. 1.

To-day has been a horrid day. I went to church with mamma and Mildred and they played the " dead march in Saul " and sang " hush blessed are the dead " for old Mr. Thomas who died suddenly, and I cried so much that mamma told Mildred to take me out. Mildred was in an awful wax when we got outside because she's gone on Mr. Amery (the curate) and wants to stare at him all the time in his night-dress, though mother says it isn't a nightdress really but is called a surplus. Mother said afterwards that if she had known sooner about old Mr. Thomas, she'd have let me stay at home, because she knew it would be " too much for my feelings " . . . . Mr. Wilcox came to Sunday dinner, and papa carved the fowl with bread source, and after that we had ginger pudding. But I couldn't eat my pudding because something awful happened just then. Mr. Wilcox said to papa, " Why, Mildred gets more like her mother every day, don't you think so?" And then before anybody could say anything, Mildred who was in a naughty mood and had been passing remarks, said cheekily, " I suppose if I grow up like mother you'll want to marry me?" " Well of course," said Mr. Wilcox. " I expect that's because you really want to marry mamma," said Mildred, getting cheekier still. " Well, of course," said Mr. Wilcox again, and I saw him wink the other eye at papa. Then Mildred said, " O you naughty

19

man, you've committed adultry." There was a dreadful shindy after that, and mamma went as red as a flannel petticoat and sent Mildred out of the room, and papa said some words in French, and I blubbed and said, it wasn't her fault, because Miss Griffin had told us in scripture that if a gentleman wanted to marry a lady who's married, it was called committing adultry. Then papa pulled a face and said, " Well of all the —!" and Mr. Wilcox patted my back and said "never mind, little man, it's a funny world," and gave me tuppence to spend tomorrow on sweets. But it was all horrid, and I wished Mildred had been a better girl, because I can't bear rows. I think papa felt sorry for us presently, because as a great treat he played the Pilgrim's Progress with us after tea in the dining room.

Feb. 2.

That night I saw Jesus again. He stood at the end of my bed and smiled at me. His lights were so lovely, all gold and pink and blue and green and yellow like the rainbow we saw through the window that time. He looked as if he wanted to comfort me for the horrid day I had. He has the most sweet blue eyes and long brown hair, and he made me feel so happy. This is the third time I've seen him, but I wish he'd come oftener. (As far back as I can remember I have been clairvoyant, and could see disembodied entities and the human aura, which I referred to as " the lights." All the same, I had never heard of clairvoyance, and imagined it was a natural faculty which everyone possessed, like the five senses. That it might be a "sixth sense" never occurred to me, and both my innocence with regard to it and the

20

faculty itself were to land me in many difficulties, as the diary reveals. During my earliest years, whenever I mentioned having " seen things " the matter was of course received with smiling indulgence on the part of my parents and ascribed to my childish imagination. But later on this attitude was replaced by something much more disconcerting.) I hated our lessons to-day. Miss Griffin was in the dumps all the time and her lights looked like a Bradford fog, worse than ever. I knew what was up. Mamma had been giving her an awful talking to about that adultry. Because when she came this morning I was leaning over the bannisters and I saw mamma come out of the library and say she wanted to speak to her. And so she went in, and they were closeted together, as pa says—and I like it because it sounds rude—for an awful long time. And then when she came up stairs her eyes were all red and she could hardly bid us good morning. She sulked all through the lessons, till Mildred asked her why she was in the dumps, though of course Mildred knew all the time. Then she began to blub and said she'd never been so badly used in her life, and told Mildred she was a horrid little mischief maker. And I felt awful because it does make me so uncomfy to see old ladies cry. (A somewhat libellous remark, as Miss Griffin could not have been more than thirty-eight.) It was all very mortifying, as Mrs. Buddle says about everything.

Feb. 4.

To-day at dinner I asked mamma if she often saw Jesus, because on my birthday I had seen him (while) in bed. And Mildred giggled and so did Janet who was handing the potatoes. I wonder why? And I wonder why mamma wouldn't tell me, but only said she was sure Jesus wouldn't want to come to little boys who weren't attentive in church, and looked about them and didn't think of what they were saying. I can't make out why mamma won't believe me when I tell her things. She always used to. Mildred says I'm dotty, but mother called me some long word to Mr. Wilcox which I can't remember. This evening papa was late again (from business) and I was very anxious because I thought he might have got run over or been murdered. Mildred told me not to be silly, but I went and prayed to God to bring him home safely all the same, and was mighty glad when I heard him come in and tap the weather-glass in the hall. (This fear that something might happen to my parents was a thing which frequently tormented my imaginative mind. The servants were largely to blame. Discussing the sensational news in the Press, they gloated over accidents and murders before "us children" in a manner calculated to make our flesh creep, as it obviously made theirs. But whilst *they* delighted in the sensation, with me it created a complex which took some years to eradicate.)

Feb. 4.

After lessons this morning when mamma was out, I repaired to the library and read a little in papa's diary, but missed out a lot of it till I came to the nice parts. In one bit it says that the servant fell down and exposed her arse. (I *would* just happen on that passage. As my father did not keep a diary, I obviously meant the diary in his bookshelves.) But as I didn't

22

know what the word means, I looked it up in the dic. and it said buttocks, which was double dutch to me. When I asked Mildred what an arse was, she said I was one myself for not knowing, and that we had ridden on them at Rhyll. But that didn't seem right either, because in the Bible, donkey is spelt ass. So this afternoon I asked Miss Griffin what buttocks were, and she said she'd never heard of them; which is all very vexing. (Strangely enough, the only term for posterior we ever used was b-t-m, hence this naivete.) Mamma and papa are asked to the vicar's to-night, and Mildred and I are asked there on Saturday, because it is Henry's birthday. I wonder if we will play hunt the slipper? . . . Mamma gave me a long talking to after lunch because she says I can never learn to be tidy. And she says papa is getting sick of telling me not to be late for breakfast and that if it happens again I shall have to be punished sevearly. Drat it all.

Feb. 5.

I asked mamma and papa at breakfast how they enjoyed themselves at the vicar's, and mamma said " Very much, thank you," and that the vicar had asked after me, which she thought was very kind of him. ("The Vicar " as my parents called him, was an imposing ecclesiastic with a black beard and a large stomach, who preached lengthy sermons in a theatrical manner.) Mildred told mamma that Janet say she thinks the Vicar rather fancies himself, and papa giggled, but mamma got very vexed, and said Janet had no bizzness to say such a thing and that Mildred was never to repeat it . . . Susan (the cook)

23

had a very red nose this evening when I went into the kitchen, and made a lot of rude noises, not the very rude ones, the others. Janet told Mildred afterwards that it was called belching. But when we went into the library to kiss papa home from the office and Mildred asked why the cook belched so much, mamma was angry and said, " I suppose you picked up that horrid word from the servants. Never let me hear you say it again, or I shall rarely have to forbid you to go into the kitchen." " Well, what do *you* call it? " said Mildred. " I don't mention such things at all," said mamma, " they are never spoken of in company." "Why not? " I asked. " *Because*——" said mamma. And papa pulled a funny face and said " I suppose I must now go upstairs and wash my hands."

Feb. 18.

We went to the dansing class this afternoon and I saw my sweetheart again. I wish I was bigger and could see her cry. Every night in bed I pretend she is crying and then I fall asleep. Mildred calls me a softie for being gone on her, because, she says, she has such silly close (clothes) and her legs are like sossages. So I gave her tit for tat and told her that *she* was a softie to be gone on our curate who has a face like a horse. And she told me a fib and said she wasn't gone on him—but I know better. Afterwards I said I was sorry and asked her to help me with my sums, but she said she couldn't, because she wanted to go to the closet. When Mildred goes to the closet, she stays there for hours. She says she hasn't been for six days because she hates that horrid stuff mamma makes us take, and so she pretends she doesn't want (require) it. I'm sure mamma would be very angry if she knew, and if she knew about me too. (I believe Buckle says somewhere in his History that the characteristics of nations may often be traced to their type of diet. If this is true, he might have made a few apt remarks about the Victorians and their fodder. All the inmates of our house were constipated, with the exception of the cat and the parrot; the consequence being that my mother and myself suffered from horrible fits of depression, my father was always complaining of liver and indigestion, the cook was afflicted with pronounced dyspepsia—though there were other causes at work—whilst the parlourmaid suffered from the most embarrassing form of flatulence. If my tomboy of a sister came off the best at the time, she was destined to suffer later on, when she grew into a nervy and delicate young woman).

Feb. 19.

I was too in the dumps to write my diary last night. When Mildred and I came back from Arnold's where we'd been asked to tea, we went to speak to mamma in the morning room, and I saw Uncle Willie sitting in papa's chair, and smiling at us. And just then papa came back from bizzness, and after he had kissed us all, was going to sit down, when I cried " Don't sit there, Uncle Willie is sitting in that chair." And mamma looked all funny, and said, " I rarely don't know what we're going to do with that child," and papa said, very cross, " What *are* you talking about, boy? Why, your Uncle Willie has been dead these two years." Then he told Mildred to take me upstairs at once. When

25

we get into the nursery, I asked her if *she* hadn't seen Uncle Willie, and she said " Of course not, you horrid little fibber." I couldn't make it out, and felt very miserable. After I was in bed, mamma came up, like she always does, to give me my hug, and said she wanted to talk to me very seriously. So she sat down, and said that naughty little boys who told such dreadful wicked stories like that about poor Uncle Willie would never go to heaven, and I must promise never never to say such things again. Then I began to cry, and said it *wasn't* a story, and I *had* seen Uncle Willie, and that it'ud be a wicked story if I said I hadn't. After that she looked at me a long time without passing any remark, and then she did a big sigh and said, " Oh very well," and went away before she had hugged me good-night. This made me so wretched that I cried still more and wished I could die. And then after I had dried my eyes on my nightgown and made it wet, all at once I saw Jesus standing by the bed all shiny like the sunset. And he smiled so sweetly and seemed to say, " forgive them for they know not what they do." Then I thought I heard him say very softly, " Be at peace," and I felt happy again, and soon went to sleep. But to-day mamma has hardly spoken to me, and it looks as if she didn't love me any more. I wish I could make it out. But I try not to mind so very much, because I know Jesus loves me and isn't displeased with me.

Feb. 21.

Henry came to tea and we played " beggar me neihbour." I think mamma likes Henry best of all my chums because the vicar is his pa. When he comes and Janet has answered the bell, mamma nearly always goes into the hall, and I hear her kind of giggling and saying, "And how is your father keeping, and your mother, and are your brothers and sisters quite well?" And then when he has gone, she comes up into the nursery and says, "Well, and what did Henry have to say?" And if he has said anything about the vicar, she wants to know all about it, because Mildred says mamma does like a bit of scandal; the word she picked up from Ethel who picked it up from her pa. But I don't believe she knows what it really means, (really again spelt rarely) because when I asked her she got cheeky, and told me to go and ask my grandmother. And so I looked it up in the dic. and it said "offence given by the faults of others." I thought that was a bit funny, so I looked up "fault", and it says, "a blemish, a wrong placing of the ball at lawn-tennis," and a lot of other things. But when I asked Mildred what balls had to do with the vicar, she said "Don't you know the vicar is a canon, and haven't you ever heard of canon balls, you dunce? And then she pulled snooks at me and laughed. I do wish Mildred wasn't such a tease.

March 1.

We went to church to-day and the organ was lovely. I wish church was all music and there were no sad sermons that make me cry. Papa doesn't often go to church on sunday mornings, because when it is a fine day he likes to go for a walk, and when it is wet he likes to read in his study. When mamma and us children come home, she tells him at sunday dinner all about

27

who was at church and who wasn't at church, and she wonders why, and all that. Mildred says grown-ups do talk about silly things sometimes. But to-day there was something else to tell papa about, because that great fat Mrs. Aldridge fainted in the prayers and it took crowds of gentlemen to take her out. I felt awful, like I always do when any body is taken ill, and had the feeling as if I'd no inside. After mamma had told papa all about poor Mrs. Aldridge, I asked mamma why her lights (aura) often went bluer when she was in church. And what do you think she said? She said to papa, " I'm beginning to wonder if there isn't something wrong with that boy's eyes." " More likely his liver," said papa. Why wont mamma tell me things when I ask her? I would like to know why there is a lot of yellow like buttercups round papa's head and only blue round mother's, though sometimes when she hugs me very hard it goes pink. And I would like to know why Mildred's lights are just a mess like the joke of a dirty egg. I've told her so too, but she says " Oh, shut up, you are dotty." But of course she is only in fun. Still, Mildred does vex me sometimes, and I would love to smack her BTM. Whenever I've asked her what *my* lights are like, she says, " Don't talk silly, you haven't got any lights." But I know she's fibbing, because when I asked Janet one day, she said they were all colours like that lovely stuffed bird in papa's glass case. (It is needless to add that I did not know that Janet was merely humouring me. Yet that I should take her seriously was not entirely illogical, having not then discovered that my capacity to see the human aura came under the heading of the super-normal. But for that

28

matter so does the capacity to compose music or play the violin like a Kreisler; yet only the ignorant would regard such gifts as pathological. Not that I consider my own modest gifts are on the same plane as genius —far from it).

March 2.

I was let off lessons this morning because Mamma took me to town to see about my eyes. A funny little man in black made me look at a big card all covered with letters, and then he stuck up bits of glass I had to stare through. When I had been doing this for a long time, I heard him say to mamma, " there is nothing to worry about, madam, the little gentleman has perfect sight." After that we went and had dinner at a restoron when we met Antie Flo, and then we came home in the train. I like going in the train, but I do wish the engine wouldn't make that horrid noise (whistle) it does make me jump so . . . . The parrot has learnt to do Susan's rude noises. I love Polly.

March 6.

A new doctor came to see me to-day and asked me all sorts of funny questions. He has whiskers and a beard which sticks out all round, and great thick specticles that make him look like an owl in my picture book. He wanted to know if I heard noises when no body was in the room. And so I said I sometimes heard mamma's voice shouting to the servants in the kitchen; and he laughed and said he didn't mean that. So I don't know what he did mean. But he was very kind, and had nice lights, though not half so lovely as Jesus's.

29

I asked if I should have to take horrid medicines like Dr. Bolton gives me, and he said, no, and that he would give me some nice little pills that tasted like sweeties. So I loved him for that and was mighty glad. Then he left the room with mamma and I heard them go into the library and shut the door where they stayed a fine long time. (My bewildered parent, having got no satisfaction out of the oculist, had called in another physician —I think he was a homeopath—in the hopes of discovering whether I was really an incorrigible little liar or was heading for the lunatic asylum. If only my mother could have investigated Spiritualism—which till the day of her death she regarded as essentially wicked—or could have known something about the rationale of clairvoyance, she *might* have come to the conclusion that her little son was neither a lunatic nor more addicted to untruthfulness than many little boys born in a highly hypocritical Age. Be that as it may, the final upshot was that the new doctor had recommended a thorough change of air, and a Hydro by the sea was advocated. But needless to say, it failed to cure my clairvoyance!).

March 9.

Oh dear, oh dear! Mildred told me to-day that Susan is going, and I shall have to say good-bye, and I know I shall blub and feel awfull. When I asked Mildred why she is going, Mildred said Janet told her she had misconducted herself, and that was all she would say. But Mildred begged and begged her to tell, so she said that Susan had come back very late from her day out last night, and when mamma and papa came home from that dinner-party they had been to, they caught her doing number 1 on the bed in the middle of all the lovely crocusses. Papa was very angry, but she only answered him back and passed a lot of rude remarks, and then was sick right in front of mamma on the walk. Mildred says Janet told her she is glad Susan is going, because she tipples, and she won't put up with it any more; that's why she makes those rude noises. And so of course I wanted to know what tipple means, and Mildred said it was when people drank too much beer and gin and stuff and got drunk. And then I said, Supposing I went and asked Susan nicely not to tipple any more, do you think mamma and papa would let her stop? And Mildred said " My Goody-Two-Shoes! you'd better not, because we aren't supposed to know anything about it, and there'd be a fine rumpus if you went and blabbed. Janet told me as a great secret." So to-night I'm very miserable because I love old Susan who is always kind to me, though her breath smells a bit nasty now and then I must say. When she goes, I think I shall hide in the closet, then I shan't have to say good-bye.

March 19.

Three clergymen came for dinner to-day, dear Mr. Wilcox, Mr. Amery who is Mildred's sweetheart, and a Mr. Finch, who has three hairs gummed over his bald head, mutton-chop whiskers, and who talked in such a silly way that I wet my nickerbockers because I tried so hard not to giggle. He put on a voice like as if he was reading the prayers all the time in church, and stuck "eh" before everything he said, and called mamma, dear lady, whenever he uttered. When she asked him, Now can't I press you to a little more mutton? he answered

" Thank you, no, dear lady "; and Mildred giggled and Mr. Wilcox winked at me. Mamma was trying not to laugh herself. In the middle of the pudding I asked Mr. Amery why clergymen always wear black, when it is such a nasty colour? And Mildred frowned at me because she's gone on Mr. Amery, and thought I ougntn't to have said that. But the others laughed, and mamma said "little boys ought to be seen and not heard," like she often says, which vexes me. But I wonder why clergymen always do wear black? because I have only seen it round people I don't much fancy. (Although I could see the auric emanations around people, I was at that time too inexperienced to know what the various colours indicated.).

March 23.

As a great treat I was allowed to go with Janet to hear Mr. Wilcox last night. He preached about prayer. Janet says she likes Mr. Wilcox's church better than our church and thinks he preaches nicer than the vicar. I like Mr. Wilcox's church too, though ours is bigger and grander. When we got home I asked mamma if she always says her prayers in the closet? And she looked very surprised and said, " Of course not; whatever makes you ask that?" So I told her Mr. Wilcox had read out in his sermon that Jesus said when we pray we ought to enter into our closets. Then I saw papa shaking (with laughter) behind his book, but afterwards he told me that in olden times, closet often meant a little room, and not the W.C. So then I said, " But if Jesus told us to go and pray in a little room by ourselves, why do we go and pray in church where there is a crowd of people?"

And papa looked at mamma, and said " Hump! there's a teaser for you." But mamma said I should understand by and by when I was older. I think it is all very provoking.

March 26.

I have been feeling very poorly all day, and wanted to cry and cry and cry. Mamma has looked concerned and asked, " Whatever is the matter?" And I could only say, " I don't know, but keep thinking of the time when you and papa and Janet and pussy and the parrot will have to die, and I don't know what I shall do." (1) I can't write any more to-night.

April 23.

I have been in bed for three weeks, and have had to have Dr. Bolton who has come every day. He says I've had jorndiss but that I'm getting better now, so I'm sitting up in bed and writing this in pencil, but will copy it in ink when I can get about again. Mr. Wilcox came to see me three times and brought me some lovely grapes, and the vicar came once and brought me a book with pictures of Jesus. But when I *see* Jesus, he looks ever so much nicer than he does in the pictures. Susan went while I was ill, so I didn't have to say good-bye, which is a comfort. I am tired now, so must stop.

April 25.

Arnold has been to tea with me, and we played Snap on my bed. I asked him about his diary, and he said he had given over keeping it long ago because it was too much sweat. So I thought I'd tell him that once

(1) *See Appendix and for all following numerals shown in text.*

33

when I said that word, mamma told me that only common people sweat, but gentlemen perspire. But Arnold said he'd often seen his father wipe himself and say, " I'm sweating like a pig " and as his father is a gentleman I think mamma must be mistaken.

April 27.

I have found out where we are going when I am well enough. Mamma says we should have gone sooner if I hadn't been so poorly. We are going to Birkdale to stay at a hydro. When I asked mamma what a hydro was, she said it was a kind of big hotel where people got water all over them to make them well. Mildred is going to stay with antie Jean at Ormskirk, and papa is going to his club at Leeds and coming to Birkdale over sundays, and I shan't have to do any more lessons for a long time. How lovely. (I heard later that the homeopath—if homeopath he was—had declared that my brains were over developed at the expense of my nerves and physique, and that a protracted holiday was indicated. It is true that I was a puny individual for my age, but although over fond of poring over books, I cannot see that I was an especially brainy child.).

Mildred thinks it is very provoking she has to go to antie Jane's, and says it is a beastly shame, because of all the ants, Antie Jane is the most particular. Papa told her at breakfast that in *her* house she'd have to mind her peas and cues. " Yes," said mamma, " and mind you do, or I shall be hearing about it." But Mildred only pouted, and said nothing. I can't say I fancy ant Jane myself very much, she has such dirty lights (a murky aura) and she always looks tight.

34

April 29.

We got here to-day. I cried an awful lot when I said good-bye to papa and Janet, but felt better as soon as it was over. I liked going in the train very much till I began to feel uncomfy because of wanting to do number 1. (There were no corridor carriages). It was lovely to look out of the windows at the cows and sheep in the fields and at the trees all out in blossom. But I don't like the tunnels because a lot of black smoke came in through the window and made a horrid smell, and I felt shy because I thought the people might think it was me. There was an old body on the seat opposite who had lovely lights, all pink and blue, and I wanted to talk to her, but thought that mamma would be vexed if I did, because she was only a common woman. (Yet judging from her aura, by no means a common *soul.*) But we smiled at each other now and then when mamma wasn't looking. (I probably did my mother a gross injustice on this occasion. Although like most Victorians, she was deplorably class-conscious, she was none the less essentially kind-hearted, and would hardly have objected to my exchanging a few pleasantries with a poor woman in a railway carriage.) When we got to Southport, a sort of omnibus met us at the station, and brought us here to the hydro (at Birkdale). Antie Jane met Mildred at Southport so that she wouldn't have to go in the train by herself to Ormskirk. I didn't blub when I said good-bye to Mildred because she isn't grown up. It is only grown-ups that make me want to cry, like Janet and mamma and papa and Mr. Wilcox, though I did nearly blub when I had to leave pussy and the poll parrot.

April 30.

I have never stayed in such a big house before and had my meals with so many people who all talk at once and make even more noise than when mamma has her day at home. Instead of servants like Janet, men hand the things, dressed up like papa when he is asked out to a grand party. But there are servants like Janet to make the beds and empty the slops called chambermaids. I asked mamma if they are called that because they clean out the jerries, but she said they weren't, because chamber means a bedroom too. Mine is called Sarah, and has a little brown mark on her cheek with three hairs sticking out. Mamma says that is a mole, but that I mustn't ever mention it to Sarah who is Welsh. I asked mamma if all Welsh people had moles, and she said, no, but that a lot of Welsh women were servants. She says that the men who hand the things at table are called waiters, because they wait on people at meals. But when I asked her why they wear swallow tails and a dicky like papa in his best, she couldn't tell me. Mamma bought me some new singlets and drawers which make me itch so that I could cry and want to scratch myself all over. I do hate being a little boy. I'm sure grown-ups aren't made to wear what they don't want to.

May 4.

I had a turkish bath to-day, and perspired like a pig. There were crowds of naked old parties sitting on chairs all round the room and looking very rum. I do think fat old gentlemen look awful with nothing on, and do hope when I'm grown up I shan't get fat and have a beard growing on my chest. After I'd got very hot, a man put me on a table and rubbed me all over, and then made me stand under a sort of umbrella and a lot of cold water came out of little holes and gave me the creeps. I don't much fancy a turkish bath, but the doctor said I must have one now and then to make me strong.

May 8.

I have made friends with a little girl my own age called Marjorie, though I think she is a naughty little kid, and her lights look like sort of dirty blood and make me feel quite sick. But mamma says she looks such a good little girl, and I heard her say to *her* mamma that she has a face like a little angel, and to me she said she would be such a nice little playmate. But if she only knew! At all events, we play together in the sandhills where there is nobody, and sail paper boats in the puddles which she knows how to make. This morning she wanted me to take down my nickerbockers. And when I said, " What is the good?" she said, " Because I want you to." So I told her I was sure mamma would be very vexed if I did. Then she said, " You would be a silly to go and tell her, I don't go and tell *my* mamma things." After that she began to hug me a lot, and said if I wouldn't do what she wanted she wouldn't play with me any more. So I said, I didn't care, I'd much sooner play by myself. And then she began to cry and called me a horrid unkind little boy. This made me cross, because I don't want to see *little* girls cry, I only want to see big girls cry. So I told her to hold her noise, though I felt sorry for her inside . . . (Hereafter follow

37

a few sentences which show that the child was obviously oversexed for her age, and an exhibitionist at that. And this was the little "angel" my unsuspecting mother had thought such a suitable playmate for her piously brought-up offspring!).

May 3.

Mamma was very put out this afternoon because I went off by myself to the shore and didn't wait for Marjorie. She said that no little gentleman behaved like that to a little lady, and that she was ashamed of me. I didn't tell her I was cross with Marjorie because she was always begging me to take down my pantaloons, I just told her I wanted to be by myself and watch the fairies playing among the stones and sea-weed on the seashore—which was true. And then she got very vexed, and said she really didn't know what she was going to do with a little boy that was so untruthful, and that she wouldn't let me read any more fairy tales if I was going to say such naughty wicked things. And so I felt very cross with mamma, and nearly cried, because it wasn't fair of her to say I had been telling fibs when she hadn't been to the shore to see for herself. And I told her so, and she said I'd have to go to bed an hour earlier as a punishment for being forward. I can't make it out, and feel very wretched. (Since my young days quite a number of reputable persons have written books testifying to the existence of little "nature spirits" known in folk lore as fairies, elves, gnomes, sylphs, etc. according to their particular function in the realm of Nature. The Irish poet, W. B. Yeats, not only believes in fairies but apparently is able to see them. (2) Many

38

Celts possess this natural gift. Had my mother only known this, I should have been saved much that bewildered and tormented my young mind). It is a rum thing but when I am very miserable about some'ut, I feel better when I have put it in my diary. I wonder why? (Without realising it, I had found "diarising" was an excellent means of "getting things off my chest." It did for me what the Confessional does for Catholics and what the psycho-analyst does for his patients.)

May 17.

We went to church this morning and papa came with us. There was a lady in our pew whose inside made funny noises, a bit like when I pull the plug in the closet, but not so loud. I giggled once and then got an awful fright because I had laughed in church, which is very wicked. An old gentleman in the next pew always smelt his top hat every time we knelt down for prayers, and I wondered what he was up to and asked papa afterwards when we were walking home. He told me he wasn't smelling his hat really, but only putting it up in front of his face. So then I asked why he didn't put it under the seat. And papa said he supposed he thought itu'd get spoilt. Then I said, "Well, why didn't he put it on the seat when he knelt down?" But papa reckoned that if he did that, he might have forgotten and sat on it when he got up. So now I know . . . I have been thinking a lot about church to-day. If I was God I wouldn't want people all over the place to recite the same things out of books every sunday, because that is silly. God made the world, so God must be very clever, and clever people don't like silly things, they like clever things. Besides,

Mr. Wilcox told me one day, that when people are really clever they don't like being told how clever they are, because it makes them uncomfy. I think poor God must feel very uncomfy on sundays.

May 20.

We had a picnic to-day. Miss Wakeham, who is Marjorie's maiden ant—mamma says when your ant isn't married she's called a maiden ant—knows how to drive a horse. And so she hired a pony-cart and took us children to a place called Freshfield, where there are some lovely woods, and we had our tea under the trees. I do like Miss Wakeham, she is so jolly and never gets tight and looks shocked when something happens like Miss Griffin. While we were driving home in the cart, the pony made some rude noises, and Marjorie giggled and I thought Miss Wakeham would be cross. But she only pulled a rum face and said, " Manners, manners!" She told us horses often did that if you give them buns, which we had done after tea because it was such fun to feed the pony with our hands. Just after we had finished tea I saw four little elves like the ones in my fairy tale book. They stared at us for a minute as if they thought us very funny, then off they ran. I nudged Miss Wakeham, and cried, " Look at the little elves." And she got excited and said, " Where, where?" but said she couldn't see them. Perhaps it's because she wears spectacles. (Needless to say that was not the reason). Marjorie didn't see them either, because just then she was behind a tree doing number 1. I wish we could go oftener to those woods and see some more little elves. They are smaller than the ones on the shore here at Birkdale, though just as rum looking.

May 21.

When papa came home this evening I was reading a book called the Pickwick Papers by Dickens, which I found in the drawing-room. But papa took it away from me because he said I should learn such a lot of bad words out of it, and he got me another book from the shelf instead, by Walter Scott. I was vexed about this, because when I saw pictures in it of men killing each other, I didn't fancy it much, though I couldn't say so to papa. I wonder why people who make up stories always want to make them up about fighting and sticking swords into each other, because it's a dirty trick, and what is the good anyhow? Besides, books about people dying make me cry, though I know it's silly, because I know they don't die really. Grandpapa and grandmamma and Uncle Willie look much nicer now when I see them (as spirits) than they did before (when they were " on earth ") . . . I had just written that down, when all at once I saw Grandpa standing there and nodding, and saying, " Quite right, my lad, and we are much happier too." And then he said " You persevere with that writing, sonny; and, mark my words, it will be printed one day, and help to lighten the darkness. Now don't you forget what your old grandpapa says!" After that he went away. But I don't know what he means by helping to lighten the darkness, though I shall persevere with my diary, I will *that.*

May 21.

Cousin Agnes came to stay for a few days, because mamma has to go home to get a new cook, so Cousin Agnes is going to see to me till mamma comes back,

41

and then we are all going home. I like Cousin Agnes, she smells so nice. Antie Jane and Mildred have been for the day. After luncheon, Mildred and I went down to the shore by ourselves, and I told her she'd see the funny little elfins. But when we got there she said she couldn't see them, and I was just a silly donkey. I think there must be something up with Mildred's eyes, because there were the elves as plain as anything . . . Mildred told me on the seashore that she simply hates Ant Jane like billyo, and says she is a beastly old cat. She told me that one day at tea she'd said, " When I'm grown up I'm going to be an actress." And Ant Jane had got into an awful wax, and said if she ever passed such a remark again in her house, she'd have to tell mamma. She said all actresses were common wicked women, and no *lady* would ever want to be an actress. This vexed Mildred so much that she forgot herself altogether and said, " All right then, I don't want to be a lady." So Ant Jane sent her up to her room for answering back. I think Ant Jane isn't fair, because papa told me that Shakespear who made up plays was one of the cleverest men that ever lived. But what'ud be the good of making up plays if it was wicked to act them? I wonder what Jesus would have to say about it?

May 25.

This morning mamma went home while I was on the shore so as I wouldn't have to say good-by. I was very glad. So now I've got Cousin Agnes all to myself . . . A rum looking party called Miss Salt— what a funny name—is staying here. She has short hair like what papa calls a rat's back, and talks in a manny voice and has an old gentleman inside her. (viz. inside her aura.) I thought this rather funny, (queer) so while we were sitting in the drawring-room before tea with Cousin Agnes, I said, " Why have you got an old gentleman sticking to you?" Then she jumped, and said, " God bless my soul! What *does* the little boy mean?" And Cousin Agnes went all red as if I'd said something rude, and sort of laughed. (with embarrassment.) And so I thought I'd better tell Miss Salt that the old gentleman had funny clothes a bit like in those pictures of Mr. Pickwick, but he wasn't near so jolly looking and had a nasty red mark (a scar) on his cheek. " Good Gracious!" she cried, " Why that was Mr.—— " and she said a name I can't remember. Then she looked uncomfy and stared at me like as if she was going to say something but thought after all she wouldn't, and uttered some'ut about washing her paws for tea, and left the room. When she had gone, cousin Agnes asked me, " Whatever made you say that to that lady? I think she is very hurt. Besides, it was such a strange thing to say. I don't know what people will think if you say things like that." So I said, " Well, it was true, so why shouldn't I?" " Because I'm afraid you'll be getting yourself into trouble one of these fine days," she said. But she wasn't very cross, so I didn't mind. (In technical terms Miss Salt was obsessed by the spirit of an old gentleman who had imposed himself on her aura and had to a considerable extent taken control. Now that the script is before me, I remember she had a deep voice and wore mannish sort of clothes and always sat with her legs wide apart and her hands resting on her knees. The obsession would easily account for this; though if she were alive nowadays her peculiarities would probably be ascribed to lesbian tendencies.)

May 26.

While I was watching William, the nice gardener who says everything is rum, Miss Salt came by, and said she was just going to take a little walk to the sea, and would I like to come with her. So I had to say yes so as not to be rude. When we got to the seashore we sat down on the lovely hot sand, and she said, " Tell me, how did you know that about the old gentleman?" So I said I could see his face in her lights. Then she asked me, what did I mean by her lights, which surprised me very much, because the old lady is not blind, and doesn't wear spectacles. So I said " Why, the colours round people, of course." Then she said. " What colours? I've never heard of that." So I reckoned this was very rum, and told her she must be short-sighted. But she said she wasn't, and I thought that so queer I said to myself, " Dear me, what is the matter with everybody?" Then I said, " You were very poorly once, weren't you? And she said " Yes; how do you know that?" So I said, " I don't know, but I *do* know (somehow.) And I know that once upon a time you had a sweetheart you was going to marry, but he had to go somewhere first a very long way off, and he got hurt, and didn't come back again." And that seemed to make her jump, and she said, " I'll tell you what, little boy?" And I said, "Yes, Miss Salt?" And she said, " Upon my word, I believe you've got second sight." But as I didn't see what she meant she said that

44

people had second sight what knew things without being told. Then I said, " Excuse me, Miss Salt " — and I'd have liked to call her Miss Pepper for fun— " but I reckon you are wrong, 'cause there are a fine lot of things I don't know, and have to ask papa or Miss Griffin. I had to ask her what is a circumcision and what it means to covet your neighbour's ox or his ass, and a lot of other things out of scripture. And that seemed to make Miss Salt laugh, and she said, " Oh I don't mean those sort of things, I mean things that have happened like me being so poorly." Then she took out of her satchel a funny old photograph, and said, " Do you know who that is?" So I said, " Why that's the old gentleman." And she said, " Quite right." And after that she gave me sixpence to buy some lollipops, and thought we must be getting back now, as cousin Agnes might be wondering what had become of me. And that was the end of that.

May 29.

Mamma has met with a new cook, so she has come back again. But I have got into trouble because Miss Salt went and told tales about me, and mamma was very angry, and said, " I am really at my wits end to know what to do with you. If there is any more of this sort of thing, your papa will have to use the slipper." (Some years afterwards, I learned from my cousin Agnes who had taken up Spiritualism, that Miss Salt had not " told tales about me," but had observed to my mother that she had a remarkable little boy who was evidently possessed of second sight. However, instead of being flattered, my devout and conventional

45

parent was horrified). Mamma locked me up in the bed room for an hour because I took liberties with Miss Salt and oughtn't to have told her about the old gentleman or anything. But I don't mind much now, because while I was there I saw Jesus again, and he smiled at me, and I am sure he wouldn't have, if I'd been really wicked.

June 1.

Mamma's friend Mrs. Croft, who lives at Southport, called for us to-day in her carriage and pair and took us to luncheon at her grand house. She is very rich and keeps a waiter, though mamma told me that men who hand the things in a private house aren't called waiters but butlers instead. I asked mamma why *we* didn't have a butler, and she said they were too expensive. Mrs. Croft has a face the colour of a suet pudding and talks very slowly, and drops her aitches, which I thought only common people did. She has something sticking to her like a crab, which looked horrid and gave me the creeps. (3) But I held my noise after the row I got into about Miss Salt, and I thought I'd better say nothing. (The unfortunate Mrs. Croft died about eighteen months later of cancer.) Mrs. Croft has a lovely musical box which I was allowed to wind up after luncheon, and it played a lot of tunes.

June 9.

We have been home nearly a week now, but I haven't written in my diary because I didn't want to. The new cook is so fat she looks all of a piece, and sometimes when she is sitting down she looks as if she might as well be standing up. Her name is Georgina and she is that red in the face that papa said he hoped she wouldn't have a fit one day. But mamma thinks she is a good-natured body, and so do I. Mildred and I were asked to the vicarage to tea yesterday and we played ball in the garden, and Dora, Henry's big sister fell down and showed her drawers. Whenever we go to the Vicar's, mamma always says, " Now remember, you are not to repeat things out of the house;"—which is a bit cool, because she always likes Henry to repeat things out of *their* house when he comes to see *us*. Mildred has taken to going to a Girls' School since the half term, and thinks herself very grand. But I am not to do any more lessons till after the summer holidays . . . Next week I've been asked to go and stay a fortnight with antie Maud and uncle John at Harrogate. I shall like that, and it will be fun playing with Basil (my cousin) though he is a year older than me, and a bit rough.

June 11.

The funny old doctor came to see me again to-day, and said I was looking better for the change of air, and mamma thought so too. After we'd been talking for a bit and he had felt me all over, mamma left the room so we should be by ourselves. Then he asked me if I still saw things. And of course I said yes, though I thought it was a funny question. Then he said very amiably, " Well now, tell me what you've seen?" So I told him I'd seen Jesus, and a lot of little elves, and then I'd seen a crab sticking to a lady, and an old gentleman inside that Miss Salt at Birkdale, and a few other things. And

47

he said, "tut tut tut, that was a funny thing to see, wasn't it?" He meant the old gentleman. And I said, yes, it was a bit rum, but he wasn't to tell mamma, because she gets so displeased when I pass remarks about people. Then he told me I needn't bother my head, because doctors could always keep a secret. After that, he said, " Do you see anything now?" So I said, " Yes, I see an old lady with white hair and ringlets, and she has a lace cap on and a lace shawl, and she is nodding and smiling at you and me. She has a sweet kind face and nice lights, and says to me " I was your mother!" And this seemed to surprise the doctor so much that he said, " Hum hah, dear me, dear me." Then mamma came back into the nursery, and the two of them went off together.

June 22.

I am at Harrogate now, and think staying with antie and uncle is most satisfactory. Antie Maud is very kind and so is uncle, who makes a lot of jokes, and jogs me up and down on his knee sometimes. When antie Maud, who is not very strong, goes shopping, she always takes a cab, and I am allowed to ride in the cab with her, which is a great treat, though I get the fidgets if she is an awful long time buying something. When we go shopping in the mornings she often invites me into the confectioners and buys me a glass of milk and a penny bun. Basil has to go to school, but we play together when he comes home. He is not a very good boy, and likes to talk about rude things and tell rude jokes he has heard at school. I suppose mamma would be vexed if she knew, but of course I shan't tell her, or she might not let me come and stay here again, and that would be very tiresome. Basil asked me to-day if I knew how babies come. So I told him Miss Griffin had said the doctor brings them in a leather bag. But when I said that, he laughed at me in a most provoking way, and said I was a booby not to know they came out of women's insides. I thought this rather a nasty idea, and told him I didn't believe it at all. But he said it was true because a boy had told him so at school . . . .

June 23.

There is a lovely old tree in uncle John's garden, and to-day I sat a long time watching a funny old gnome who lives inside it, like one of the gnomes in my fairy-tale book. He has great long thin legs and wears a red cap, though the rest of him is like the colour of the trunk of the tree. Sometimes he comes out of his tree and goes prancing about in the grass and looking so funny that I want to giggle, but was afraid I might make him offended. (4) When I spoke about the old gnome to Basil, he poked fun at me, and said there were no such things, and I was a little ass to believe such fiddlesticks. I can't make it out, and wished I knew what ails everybody.

June 23.

To-day I asked old James, the gardener, about the gnome. And he said, " Well, master, if I was your age there's no telling what I'd see, but I'm getting old, and my eyes aren't what they used to be."

June 26.

A clergyman called Mr. Ramsbottom came to Antie

Mauds for luncheon to-day, and I am mighty glad Basil was asked out to a chum's, because if he'd been there I'm sure we'd have giggled. This Mr. Ramsbottom talked an awful lot, and Antie Maud who is such a polite lady, kept saying, " O yes, Mr. Ramsbottom. O indeed, Mr. Ramsbottom. Fancy that, Mr. Ramsbottom, is it really, Mr. Ramsbottom," and all the rest of it, till I nearly wet my knickerbockers trying not to burst. When Mr. Ramsbottom now and then passed a remark to me I thought it'ud do if I said sir, because I couldn't take it upon myself to say Mr. Ramsbottom, though mamma did tell me I ought always to say the person's name when I answer back or it isn't polite. Mr. Ramsbottom talked about churches he had been to see where there were some rude screens, and I thought it very funny there should be anything rude in a church, but didn't like to ask questions. He told Antie Maud she ought certainly to go and see them if she ever got the chance, which I reckon was a rum thing for a clergyman to say to a lady about something that's rude. And the funny thing is that Mr. Ramsbottom is a bit lady-like himself. He talks in rather a lady's voice, and does funny things with his hands, and sort of sniggers when there isn't much to snigger about. Of course I shouldn't like to hurt poor Mr. Ramsbottom, but somehow I don't fancy him very much.

June 24.

I thought I'd enquire of Uncle John about those screens, and he laughed and laughed so much I was afraid he was going to explode. He said they weren't rude at all, though they may sound rude, because the word is spelt rood and really means a cross. So now I suppose I did that Mr. Ramsbottom a wrong when I thought he wasn't behaving himself nicely with Antie Maud. I think Uncle is a jolly old chap, and wish I could stay longer, but mamma is coming to take me home to-morrow, drat it all!

June 26

Mamma fetched me home yesterday. I hated saying good-bye to Antie Maud and Uncle. How I wish I was made different; other children don't blub when they have to say good-bye. It is so mortifying. Perhaps if I pray to Jesus he will help me . . . . I am in disgrace to-day. Arnold came to play with me in the garden this morning, and we ate a lot of goozeberries off the trees, and I got awful stomackake and messed my pants before I could get to the closet. Janet only laughed, but mamma was that angry, because she said I'd no bizzness to pick goozegogs without asking first. I hate being a little boy, I want to be grown up. Grown-ups don't have to ask every time they want to do something, and if they get collywobbles they are not punished, but every body says they are sorry, and poor thing . . . . Mildred has got very uppish since she goes to school, but she has made friends with a big girl called Nancy Todd and brings her to our house, and I fell in love with her first go. I don't think of Florrie any more now, I think of Nancy all the time instead.

June 29.

Fancy that now! Mr. Wilcox arrived to-day in a cab. He is poorly, and the doctor said he must go to bed, and as there is no one to see to him properly in his rooms, mamma asked him to come and be ill in our house. I am sorry he is poorly, but I'm jolly glad he is here. When I asked mamma what was up with him, she said, " O nothing very serious," and put me off with that. But she must have told Janet, because Janet told Mildred, who told me, that he had a carbunkle somewhere. I wonder why it is called that, because mother wears a brooch with a carbunkle which papa gave her at Christmas. I think Mr. Wilcox's carbunkle must be on where he sits down, because when I went to say how do you do to him before he got undressed, I saw a sort of black cloud in his lights just there. (5) But I thought I'd better say nothing for fear he'd feel shy.

July 1.

I go and sit with Mr. Wilcox when he isn't too tired, and he reads out poetry to me in bed. I love poetry and would like to make up some myself when I'm older. But I don't like sad poetry about people dying, because it makes me want to cry; though I know they don't die really, else how should I see them as I often do. I saw (the spirit of) Uncle Willie again in the dining-room to-day, but said nowt to mamma, because last time she got in that wax and gave me such a talking to I still can't make out why. And come to that, I can't make out why I mind so much when people go to heaven. I reckon it's because every body gets so sad and cries, and then I feel awful and want to cry too, like when I have to say good-bye . . . . Mr. Wilcox's carbunkle *is* on his B-T-M, he told me himself as a great secret, so I was right. He made a joke though, and said he couldn't sit down and

52

he couldn't stand up and he couldn't lie on his back, so he was in a fine fix and all. He said he'd like a few bumptious people to get a carbunkle on their bums, because that'ud soon take 'em down a peg or two, though I wasn't to tell any one he'd said so. I love Mr. Wilcox better than all the clergymen we know; he's so amiable and comes out with naughty things just now and then.

July 3.

The doctor came to lance Mr. Wilcox this morning. Mildred told me it hurts awfully to be lanced, so I went out into the garden so as I shouldn't know when poor Mr. Wilcox was being hurt so much . . . . Mamma got a letter from cousin Agnes to-day, and there was a little letter inside for me too. While I was reading it, I don't know why, but somehow I felt that cousin Agnes is going to get married soon. But when I told Mildred, she said, " What rubbish." So I said, " You can say what you like, but I know, Cousin Agnes has got a sweetheart who is spooney on her, and it won't be long before we hear they're engaged." " Well if you want to know," said Mildred, " Uncle Henry wouldn't let Cousin Agnes marry the gentleman she *was* sweet on, and that was only two months ago, so she can't have a new sweetheart already." " Don't you be too coackahoopy," said I, " she thought she was sweet on the last gentleman, but she's much sweeter on this one." "O shut up!" said Mildred, " and don't talk about what you know nothing about." Then she said, " I know somebody who's sweet on somebody." " Well who?" said I. " You're sweet on Nancy," said Mildred. This vexed me very much, because if she goes and tells Nancy, she'll laugh at me and think I'm a silly little boy. But when I asked Mildred not to, she said she'd please herself. I do think she is mean, I do that.

July 4.

Mr. Wilcox feels better to-day, now that he's been lanced behind. I am so glad . . . . I told mamma I thought cousin Agnes was going to be married. And she looked very surprised, and said, " What in the world makes you say that?" And so I said, I had the feeling. Then she said, " Little boys oughtn't to have feelings— at least, not of that sort. Surely she said nothing to you in that letter?" So I told her she hadn't. " Go and bring the letter," said mamma. And I had to trot up-stairs and rummidge in my drawers to find it. When I'd shown it to her, she said, " You're not to say things like that; a nice lot of mischief you might make." But I think it isn't fair, because I *was* right, and mamma might have been decent and not pretended I wasn't. And now I've found her out. Fact is, papa has been away for two nights on bizzness. But when he came back this evening and went into mamma in the study, he forgot to shut the door, and just as I was going to kiss him home, I heard mamma let the cat out of the bag. I heard her say, " O, you'll be surprised to hear Agnes has got engaged, but it's not to be given out yet." Then she saw me and looked much annoyed. After I had kissed papa, she said, " Did you hear what I was just saying to your father?" So I had to say yes. " Well," she said, "now understand this is not to be mentioned to any one. Do you hear? If it goes any further I shall be very angry, and so will Cousin Agnes . . . And now you can run along." After that I came out into the garden, and am writing my diary in the arbour. I nearly always write my diary out of doors when the weather is fine and warm, I do love the smell so, when the flowers are out, and I love the feel of the air on my face. I wish I didn't have to wear clothes, it must be lovely to feel the air all over. But I am disappointed in mamma, because she told us one day that it's as naughty to act a fib as to tell one—and then she goes and does it herself, and scolded me on top (of it all) for saying what she knew was true all along. I call that mean, I do. Ah well, I feel better since I have written all this down.

July 8.

Mamma told us to-day that we are all going to a place called Keswick, in the lakes, for our summer holidays, and that perhaps Mr. Wilcox is going to come with us. What fun. We are off on the 28th. Mr. Wilcox is up now and is able to sit down, so he played the piano to me to-day. When I hear music, I see lovely things and sort of have the most lovely dreams. I am sure there must be a lot of music in heaven, though I don't believe people sit all day and play on harps, else how could I have seen Uncle Willie and Grandpapa and the like. They didn't have harps—and come to that— they didn't have wings either like pictures of angels in the goody-goody books. Georgina (the cook) who goes to chapel, says that when good people die, they are turned at once into angels, and sit round God singing hymns for ever and ever. But how could she go and say that when she must have seen people (spirits) who weren't sitting round God? (I had still failed to grasp

55

that everyone could not see spirits, or better said, was not possessed of "astral sight.") I was just going to ask her, when mamma came into the kitchen, so I thought I'd better not, as she gets so angry when I mention such things. I wonder if I shall ever know why? It isn't as if they were rude . . . . Mr. Wilcox is so clever on the piano that he can play everything by heart, and can even make up things as he goes along. I am going to ask mamma if I can't have music lessons after the holidays.

Keswick. Aug. 4.

We have been here a week now, and I have seen crowds of fairies and elves and mannikins and gnomes, and it's simply lovely. But papa will take us such long walks that sometimes I feel that tired I could almost cry. Mamma told him it was too much for me, but he said it would do me good, and that all that's the matter with me is that I don't get enough exercise. Papa is cracky on exercise, and reckons that if he had the time to take plenty of exercise he would never have the liver. Of course Mildred doesn't care how much she walks. I believe if she had to walk round the world she wouldn't mind. I like it best when we go in a boat on the lake, though I would rather papa didn't row, because he perspires so much and gets all niffy. Mr. Wilcox doesn't get like that and smell of mutton chops. But perhaps it's because papa is so much fatter.

Aug. 8.

I don't like the feeling of my bedroom in our lodgings, it gives me the creeps. Sometimes I see a horrible old woman who comes and looks at me in bed. She wears old fashioned clothes, and looks a bit like that witch in my story book, and has a bad, wicked face. I wanted to ask mamma to send her away, but am afraid to say anything to mamma now for fear she'll get angry. But last night when Mr. Wilcox came up to read me a story, which he sometimes does as a great treat, I told him about the old woman, and begged him to shoo her off. He seemed a bit surprised at first, but then he said, " I'll tell you what. Let's say a prayer, and if she's really a naughty old witch, she won't like that and she'll skidaddle." So he knelt down and asked Jesus to save us from all evil and fear—though I can't remember just the words he said. And then when I opened my eyes, I saw Jesus for a minute all shining and lovely, and his lights were so bright that I couldn't see the old woman any more. And when he had gone, she had gone too. Mr. Wilcox told me afterwards that next time I thought I saw anything that frightened me, I should pray to Jesus like that, and then I'd feel better. But come to think of it, I wonder why he said, " The next time you *think* you see anything to frighten you?" because it looks as if he reckoned it was all my fancy, which of course it isn't. Or is it perhaps that when there's anything horrid, he wants me to think it's only fancy so as I shan't be afraid.

Aug. 11.

A lady and gentleman turned up at our lodgings yesterday, and papa said they must be on their honey moon, because he saw the man bringing in their luggage, and it looked all brand new. They are in the

57

bedroom next to mine, and they woke me up once in the night and gave me a nasty fright. I think one of them must have fallen out of bed or something, because I heard an awful bump on the floor, and noises as if someone was hurt, which gave me that nasty feeling in my middle, like when a lady faints in church and has to be taken out. At breakfast this morning I told them all about it, and asked why people sleep together when they get married, didn't they feel very shy? And mamma blushed and sort of giggled, and papa laughed a bit and said a long French word to Mr. Wilcox which sounded like enfongterreeble or some such thing. But they wouldn't tell me why, and only said I'd know lots of things by and by when I was grown up. I do wish they wouldn't always say that; it is so provoking. Besides—they can say what they like, I bet when I *am* grown up I shan't want to go getting into the same bed with a lady; I should feel much too mortified . . . .

Aug. 23.

We have had a lot of wet days, which has been very tiresome, because mamma won't let me go out when its pouring with rain. But to-day it cleared up after tea, and there were some lovely clouds with beautiful fairies in them which I watched through the window. They made the clouds into all sorts of funny shapes like castles, and some of the clouds they made into things like huge funny looking animals. I saw a great big fairy on top of one of the hills, and it had colours like in the rainbow. A few of the hills I've seen here have these fairies on them, and I think they are quite entrancing, as Antie Maud says about everything she

58

likes . . . Mr. Wilcox told me there used to be a lot of poets in the Lakes, and one special one called Wordsworth, and he recited bits of his poetry to me. I wish we lived in the lakes, I don't want to go home. But then of course I should want Arnold and Henry and Mr. Wilcox to live here too, because if they didn't I should miss them ever so much, I would indeed.

Aug. 28.

We have come home. The parrot has picked up Georgina's cough and the loud way she breathes. It is very funny, but I think she is rather vexed, because it sounds as if Polly was poking fun at her. Mamma says that next month I am to go to Miss Frampton's School for girls and boys. I asked her if there were any big girls there, and she said, yes, but there were no big boys. I wonder if I shall like it; though I would much sooner go to school than have a governess again like Miss Griffin. Mamma was a bit poorly to-day and couldn't go shopping, so she told me to run to the butcher's and bring back a pound and a half of the best stake. I do hate stake, but I said I'd fetch it all right, though she'd have to wait, because I wanted to go to the closet first. Then mamma said, "I've told you over and over again that you mustn't say that. You must say, please may I leave the room. Why, people will wonder where you've been brought up. Or if you are asked out, you must say, please may I wash my hands." So I said, "But supposing I don't want to wash my hands, that will be telling a fib." "Not at all," said mamma, "you should always wash your hands after you've been to that place." Of course I know mamma is very kind and good and religious and all, but she does annoy me sometimes, what with what I'm allowed to say and not allowed to say. If I tell the truth like I did about Uncle Willie, I get into a row, and if I don't tell the truth I get into a row, so I might as well hold my noise and say nowt . . . . Mildred had Nancy to tea to-day, and I am awfully in love with her, and imagine her face all the time.

Aug. 30.

This morning we went to church. The Vicar has gone for his holidays, so a Mr. Grub preached instead. I am glad I am not called Grub, it makes me think of worms. He is a rum old party. He says some words, then he shuts his eyes and pulls an awful face while he's thinking what to say next. I nearly got the giggles. The church has been done up while we were away, and smelt of varnish. It was so hot this morning that the Miss Wigans' boddices stuck to the pew. When Miss Mabel Wigans kneels down, her stays creak. Mr. Wigans makes rum noises in his chest. Mother says he suffers from assma, poor man. I am glad the Vicar was away, because I'm always afraid he'll preach a sad sermon. To-day I was thinking that I never see Jesus in church. I wonder why? But I suppose he can't be in all the churches at once, and perhaps one day it will be our turn.

Date missing.

I went to school to-day. There are 3 Miss Framptons. There is Miss Jessie who teaches the big girls, and Miss Enid who teaches the younger girls and

the boys, and I am in her class, and then there is *Miss*
Frampton, the head mistress, though a fat boy called
Charlie Baines told me that she keeps very much to
herself. But if a boy is very naughty he gets sent to
her and she gives him the cane. Miss Enid was decent
enough to-day and didn't get in a wax, but I don't like
her lights somehow and think she is very frightning.
I have the horrid feeling that I shall hate the school,
and that Miss Enid can be very nasty if one takes any
liberties.

Oct. 5.

A girl in our class had to recite a piece of poetry
called Little Jim, and it was so bad I began to cry.
And Miss Enid got very cross, and said, "what are you
making that noise for?" So I said I couldn't help it,
because the piece of poetry was so mournful. And she
said crossly, "Don't be silly, or I shall have to punish
you." And the other children sniggered at me for being
such a booby, and the boys made fun of me in the
playground afterwards and called me a crybaby. I think
Miss Enid is a hard unkind old maid; she is nearly
always cross, and when she gets into a real wax it's
simply ghastly, and my heart goes all queer and does
pitterpat. Mildred and I are to have music lessons from
a lady called Froyline Heffner. She is German, and
mamma says she plays beautifully. I am very glad, but
hope she won't be such a crosspatch as Miss Enid, or
I don't know what I shall do?

Oct. 7.

To-day is my birthday. Mother gave me that box

I wanted to lock up my diary in, and father gave me a Waterbury watch, which is grand, and Mildred gave me a box of tools, which I reckon mamma paid for, though nothing was said about that, and I pretended it was mighty decent of her to spend a particle of her pocket money on such a nice present to her thorn in the flesh. Janet gave me a box of lovely sweets with a big hug, and cook made me a scrumpscious birthday cake all covered with pink, and my name embroydered on it. We had a tea-party with Henry and Arnold as the guests of honour, and upon my word, it was all very enjoyable and the whole funkshon a great success. I'm feeling a bit done up now and shall not write any more to-night.

Oct. 8.

Before I went to sleep last night I was thinking of grandpa a bit. Then suddenly I saw him at the bottom of the bed. He smiled and said he wished me many happy returns. So I asked him how he knew it was my birthday? And he said he sort of knew it from my thoughts. I love old grandpa, he feels so kind, though of course not as lovely as Jesus. I wonder how much dead people like grandpa can see? I wonder if they see us when we are having our bath or in the closet? I am sure mamma would be very put out if grandpa or Uncle Willie was to turn up while she was in one or tother place. But I suppose neither of them would do that, because it would be rude. I don't think *nice* dead people come where they are not welcome. It is only the nasty ones like that horrid old woman I saw in the lakes.

I can't bear school, and am in such a funk of **Miss Enid** that when I have to say my French verbs or a piece of poetry they all go out of my head, though I know them quite well at home, and my heart goes ticking away as fast as Janet's (alarum) clock. Sometimes **Miss Enid** is that waxy she won't let us go to the closet when we want to. But to-day a thing happened which paid her out grand, though it made me feel awful. A boy called Jimmy Cole said, " Please, **Miss Enid**, may I leave the room?" And **Miss Enid**, who was in an extra pet this morning said, " No, you may *not* leave the room." Then after we had gone on with our lessons a bit, Jimmy Cole did number one on the floor, and **Miss Enid** had to go and wipe it up with the towel she uses to wipe the blackboard with. By gum, wasn't she in a rage. Yet she couldn't say much to Jimmy, because it was her own fault. But when we took up our exercise books to show her, if we had made any mistakes, she threw them down on the floor for us to pick up, and said we were all enough to try the patience of Job.

Oct. 20.

I like Froyline Heffner. She is fat and looks a bit like a cook, but she doesn't frighten me at all, and I do my best to please her. She has hair like straw, and round red cheeks and blue eyes, and she sticks out a lot in front and has fat little fingers that remind me of sossages. She told me that the men who made up the best music were all German, and recited some of their names. But I am only allowed to play five finger exer-

cises and scales all this term, which is rather vexatious.
Mamma calls her a nice motherly body, and said something about her having a hard struggle. Papa hasn't
seen her, so I don't know what *he* would say. Though
he doesn't mind me having music lessons, he thinks
music is silly, and says he can't tell the difference
between God save the Queen and Pop goes the Weezle.
I am not allowed to practice my exercises when he is
at home, neither is Mildred, because he says it gives
him the fidgets and he can't read his books with that
going on.

Nov. 2.

How I hate Mondays when I have to go back to
school after Saturday and Sunday. As soon as I get
into the schoolroom now I have the pitterpats and that
awful feeling in my middle, and when I get home I don't
want to eat any dinner. Mamma has been asking what
is the matter with me, because I look so white and am
off my food. So at last I told her I thought it was
Miss Enid, and that she gave me the jimjams, and then
I began to blub, I felt so miserable. Mamma thinks
perhaps I only fancy it's Miss Enid, and that there may
be something else wrong with me. But I know better.
Last night in bed I saw Grandpa, and he said, " You'll
soon be seeing the doctor. Be sure and tell him about
your schoolmistress. It is very important that you
should. Now don't forget." Then he smiled and nodded
like I remember he used to do when I was quite little,
and after that he went away. But mamma has never
said anything about me seeing the doctor.

Nov. 5.

To-day is Guy Faulkes day, so papa was awfully decent and brought home a lot of fireworks from business, and let them off before my bed time with Janet. And mamma and Mildred and I looked through the study window, and it was great fun . . . .

Nov. 6.

Grandpapa was right, and the doctor came to-day. Mamma was in the room at first, and I didn't like to tell him about Miss Enid but then some body called about a subscripshun or something and mamma had to leave us to ourselves for a bit. So I told him about the awful feeling I got in my middle, and about my heart going pitterpat and all, because grandpa had told me to tell him, though I didn't say about grandpa, as I thought I'd better not. When mamma had finished paying her subscripshun and the party had gone, she came back again. And after a bit she told me I could run along upstairs. But the doctor sat a long time talking to her, I know, because his carriage was there for ages. I could see it out of the nursery window.

Nov. 7.

I saw the old gentleman (my grandfather) again last night. And he sort of giggled, and said, "*We* sent that person along for the subscription (I have corrected the spelling) just then to get your mother out of the room, but you mustn't say anything about it." Then he said, "Cheer up, my lad, *we* are looking after you, and soon you will hear there will be no more school." And so I felt very happy and went off to sleep. Froyline gave me my lesson to-day. I have to learn the names of the great musicians by heart, so she wrote them down for me on a piece of paper, four of them to start with. Then she played me a little piece by each of them. It was simply ripping, and while she was playing I saw the most lovely things. Froyline says that she plays to me because she wants me to hear some good music. She told me the greatest musician that ever lived was a man called Beethoven. I do love my music lessons, and think Froyline is so aimable that I love her too. Miss Enid was quite decent this afternoon by way of a change. Sometimes I feel sorry for her, because it must be so awful to be always in a wax. I know I hate being in a wax myself.

Nov. 8.

Hurray, I don't have to go to school any more. What a relief. I could jump up to the ceiling, I could indeed. (Apparently the doctor had informed my mother that I was suffering from nervous dyspepsia, brought on, or at any rate aggravated, by Miss Enid's severities. He also told her that my heart was none too good, and advised her to withdraw me from the school. It seems that already several parents had complained of Miss Enid's methods, and had withdrawn their children from her untender care; so I was not the only one. She was never really suited to be a school-mistress, was not fond of children, and owing to some unhappy love affair had become a hard and embittered woman. He intimated to my mother that had she asked his advice in the first place, he would have strongly advised her against sending me to that school. Nowadays I think Miss Enid

66

would have been suspected of leanings towards **sadism**. Or it may be that she revenged herself on life by " taking it out " of her unfortunate charges). I wonder what will happen to me next? I don't much want to have Miss Griffin back again, though she didn't frighten me like Miss Enid, but she was so serious and never laughed at anything.

Nov. 17.

There is something up with mamma. She has been staying in bed for breakfast. And to-day when we were in the dining room she was sick in the coal-box because she couldn't get to the closet in time. When mother is ill I am always frightened she is going to die. But Mildred says that when people are going to die they get very thin, so perhaps it's all right, because mamma is not getting thin, she is getting all fat about the middle like the Vicar. I think it's a great pity, because she doesn't look so nice.

Dec. 23.

Christmas will soon be here. I am running a lot of messages for mamma. She is giving presents to crowds of people, and I have to go and hand them in at the doors. She sent me with a huge parcel to the Vicarage. Mamma says she'll be glad when Christmas is over, but I shan't. She has got still fatter, yet always seems to be tired now. I can't make it out.

Dec. 26.

Yesterday was Christmas Day, and we all went to church in the morning, but the Vicar said something sad

in his sermon which made me cry a bit. Mr. Wilcox
came for our Christmas dinner, and we had turkey and
sossages and plum pudding and raisens and armonds
and oranges and things. I got lots of presents, but the
lovliest of all was a musical box from Mr. Wilcox which
plays tunes like Mrs. Croft's. The postman didn't come
till three o'clock, and papa gave him a shilling for his
Christmas box. Mamma got hundreds of cards and
stuck them up all over the drawring-room mantlepeace,
and I got some nice cards too. The house looked ever
so magnificent, because Janet and Mildred and I had
stuck up holly all over the shop on Christmas Eve, and
we stuck a bunch of mistletoe in the hall. After
Christmas dinner Mr. Wilcox played games with us and
we had great fun. In the evening he dressed up as
Father Christmas and talked like a very old gentleman
and papa laughed a lot and was quite frisky. But
mamma was not up to the mark, and didn't seem to
enjoy herself as much as we did. Mr. Wilcox went into
the kitchen and gave both the servants a Christmas box,
and Mildred and I gave them presents, and they gave
us something too. As it was Christmas Day I was
allowed to stay up longer and have supper in the dining
room, and before I went to bed, Mr. Wilcox showed us
some conjuring tricks after he had played some Christmas carols on the piano. To-day I feel a bit squeamish,
but nothing like what I used to feel at school. Crumbs!
how thankful I am that Miss Enid is no more. Just
as I was trying hard to go to sleep last night, I saw
Jesus. He said he had come to give me a special
Christmas blessing, and after that I felt all peaceful like,
and fell asleep.

Jan. 1.

I have got a tutor now. He comes at a quarter past nine till a quarter to one, and at eleven we stop lessons for a quarter of an hour to have a glass of milk and some biscuits. His name is Mr. Patmore, and he is rather old, and I like him very much, and am not a bit afraid of him, because he seems so nice and kind. He has white hair parted in the middle and a little beard like a nanny goat, and a funny humorous look in his eye, so different to Miss Enid. His nose is a bit like the parrot's, only of course it isn't black, and he smells of pipe. He said he was sure we'd get on together like a house on fire, and I replied that I was sure we would too. He doesn't come in the afternoon, but I am to do some lessons by myself to show him the next day. I shall try and do my best to please him, because I don't want him to feel disappointed in me. When Janet had brought up the milk and biscuits and gone away again, he asked me to show him where the W. C. was. "It's always as well to know the geography of the house," he said; which made me laugh, because I always thought geography had to do with maps. Before he left for home he patted me on the back and said, "Well, keep up your pecker, old man, and do your lessons well, and we'll make a great scholar of you in no time." I am so happy in Mr. Patmore, because if papa had made me go to another awful school with great rough boys who knock one about, I don't know what would have become of me. (Even at Miss Frampton's I had been the victim of a lot of bullying by physically stronger boys who took a delight in tormenting me.) When papa came home this evening, he said, "Well, and how did you get on with your tutor?" So I said I thought he was all that was most desireable. And mamma and papa both laughed, and mamma said, "Where *does* he pick up these expressions?" But papa said he was glad to hear I liked Mr. Patmore, and that he had told him he must be firm with me, but mustn't get cross and frighten me.

Jan. 19.

I wish God had never made winter. It has been so dark all day we had to have the gas, and there's a smelly fog outside, and I have got chillblains and feel that cold I don't know what to do. The only nice cosy place is in the kitchen with its big fire and smell of new bread. I wish I could live in the kitchen, it is a bit like a room in a cottage and I like that. When Mr. Patmore arrived to-day, he said, "Dear me, dear me, this weather is appalling, this is what's called a darkness which can be smelt." If Mr. Patmore doesn't much care for a thing, he says it's appalling, and when he likes a thing he says, "That's most satisfactory." But even when he says a thing's appalling, there is a sort of look in his eye as if he thought it was not so awful after all, and perhaps rather a joke. Of course when I make a lot of mistakes in my exercises he doesn't think it a joke then and looks a bit sad, which makes me feel ashamed of myself. When that happens, he says, "Hum - well - a bit disappointing to-day. We must try and do better than that, eh?" But when he's pleased, he says, "Ah that's the style — most satisfactory." And then of course I feel very happy. Miss Enid never said anything nice like that even when we made no mistakes at all, so what was the good of trying to please her, the old crosspatch. How lucky I am to have met with Mr. Patmore, I am really.

Jan. 25.

I said to Mildred to-day, " I do wish mamma hadn't got so fat, she's as fat as Georgina now." And Mildred said, " Oh well, she'll soon be thin again." " How do you know that?" said I. " Never you mind," said she, " I do know. A girl told me at school." " Go on with you," I said. Come to think of it, there's something a bit funny about mother's lights too, though I can't quite make out what . . . So I thought I'd ask Mildred if she had noticed anything. " What," she said, " do you mean to say you still pretend to see your silly lights? I thought you'd got over all that nonsense. I think you're cracked, or else you're the greatest fibber I've ever struck." " Fibber yourself," said I, " unless you're as blind as a bat." " Oh, go and boil your head," she cried. Mildred hasn't learnt any better manners since she's been at school. She ought to have had a bit of Miss Enid to take her down a peg, she ought that. Me a fibber indeed!

Feb. 2.

It is a queer thing, but I am to go and stay with Auntie Maud for a week, and when it isn't holidays and all. Auntie Maud is coming to fetch me on Thursday. Of course I like going to stay at Harrogate ever so. But I know what it'll be—I shall blub when I have to say good-bye to Mr. Patmore, and he *will* think me a jackanapes. I asked mamma why this thusness, and she said, " A change would do me good." But that can't be the real reason, because Mildred is being shunted too . . . I at least thought Janet would tell me something, but not she. " Ask me no questions and I'll tell you no lies," was all the answer I got. But she did say, when I got back I might find a lovely surprise. Somehow, though, I have a feeling that the surprise won't be as lovely as Janet wants to make out.

Feb. 3.

I thought I had better tell Mr. Patmore I always hated saying good-bye, seeing as I am off to Harrogate to-morrow, and that I generally blubbed, which made me feel so ashamed of myself. And he said I needn't feel so ashamed, because a lot of people didn't like saying good-bye, and if I got upset, he'd simply take no notice and then perhaps I wouldn't mind so much, and in any case it was only for a week. So I felt much relieved, and was glad I had told him beforehand. We have been reading bits of Shakespear and Dickens together. I love David Copperfield and can say some of it by heart.

Feb. 8.

Here I am at Harrogate. Auntie makes quite a fuss of me, and I have a lovely fire in my bedroom, and like to watch it when I'm in bed. Sometimes I can see the fire fairies as they leap about in the flames. There is a funny old gentleman staying for just two nights besides me. He is a bit like a big dog and sort of grunts. He grunts whenever he sits down, and sometimes he grunts instead of saying yes. His name is Mr. Potts, and he hasn't much to say for himself but sits all glum puffing at his cigar. I like the smell. He knows how to blow rings, and is very clever at it. Papa tries to blow rings too sometimes, but does not meet with much success. We had some sleet to-day, and the weather is appalling. I wish the winter would hurry up and be over, I couldn't go out to-day at all. But I did write to Mr. Patmore because he said he expected a letter from me. He wants me to learn to write good letters. He says that to write good letters is a compliment. (I think he must have said "an accomplishment.") This house is warmer than ours, which is very satisfactory. But it makes me wonder what is going on at home. Something tells me inside that mamma is very poorly, and that makes me afraid she's going to die, yet somehow I know she's not going to die. (On this very day, my sister was born, and my mother had a pretty bad time of it.) Yesterday I went in the garden for a little while. That gnome is still in the old tree, but he didn't come out and prance about the lawn. Perhaps he is not partial to the cold. Who shall say? I am supposed to be going home on Friday. Well, we shall see. What I think is, a letter will come and I shall stay till next week; but I don't know why.

Feb. 10.

Auntie has allowed me to take out an old chair and sit in the greenhouse, though she laughed, and said she thought it a funny place to choose. But I like it because it's so warm, and I love the smell. So I go there and take a book to read. Sometimes the old gardener comes

73

in to do something to the flowers, and we have a chat while he waters and all. I told him that the gnome was still there all right. And he said, "You don't say." "Yes," I said, "he's still there, there's no doubt about it." "Well," said he, "it's a fine old tree, but we shall 'ave to do a bit of lopping one of these days, we shall that." "But you won't cut down the tree?" said I, feeling quite nervous, "because if you did that, I think it would break the little chap's heart. He seems so proud of his tree." "Set your mind at rest, master, we shan't do that," said he, "we shall only cut off some of the top branches, and they'll sprout all the merrier." "I'm glad to hear that," said I. And he laughed and said something about me being a rum'un . . . . Auntie Maud has just told me she's had a letter from papa, and that I shan't be going home till next week. And fancy! I've got a little sister; and when Auntie told me that, she seemed quite excited. "How old is she," I asked. "How old?" said Auntie, looking very surprised, "why she's only a tiny baby." "Oh I see," said I, "I merely wanted to know, because if doctors bring babies in a bag, why must they be always the same age? Why can't they keep them for a bit like people keep eggs?" And Auntie seemed to think that very funny, and laughed a lot. "Well, any way," she said, "aren't you pleased?" And so I said I wasn't so sure, I'd have to think about it a bit, as I didn't much fancy a tiny baby about the place; they slobbered and squawked and smelt. When mamma had made me kiss that baby of Mrs. Stick-in-the-Mud's, I thought it appalling. "'Pon my word, you are a caution," said

Auntie. I wonder why everybody thinks me such a caution, and what is a caution anyhow?

Feb. 11.

To-day Auntie Maud said I ought to sit down at once after breakfast and write a nice letter to papa and mamma and tell them how pleased I am to have got a lovely little sister. But I said, "How can I say that, when I reckon she's as ugly as anything if other babies I've seen are anything to go by? And come to that, I'm *not* very pleased, so how can I say I am." And this seemed to stump Auntie a bit, though she was very nice and didn't get cross. "Well," she said, after she'd rattled her brains for a minute, "I'll tell you what we'll do. I'll make up something for you to write, and then you can add what you like afterwards about other things." "Very well, Auntie," I said, "that'll be most satisfactory." At which she laughed a bit, but then sat down and wrote me out something in pencil. The end of it was that I put pen to paper and told mamma and papa that I congratulated them both on the new edition to the family, and hoped the new little sister would grow up to be a joy to them and a comfort in their old age. And then I told them that I was enjoying myself very much at Auntie Maud's and Uncle John's and that they were so kind, and all the rest of it. When I told Basil (my young cousin) about the new sister, and that mamma had been getting very stout and all, he jeered at me and said, " Perhaps you'll believe now that doctor's don't bring babies in their bags? Ant Fanny (my mother) got fat because she had a baby inside her, and it hurts like sin when it comes out, so they shunted you and Mildred, because there's no end of a fuss when some one has a baby." I thought this all rather horrid, but perhaps Basil is right; though why has every body told me such awful lies?

Feb. 17.

I am back home again. Mamma is in bed and looks very poorly. She has got a nurse, and there's another nurse to see to the baby. I have to have my lessons now in papa's study. Well, I rather like that, but I think the baby's an ugly looking concern, and so does Mildred. Janet and Georgina and the two nurses pretend it's lovely, and make noises over the thing like turtle-doves. How women do go on when there's a baby in the place, they even pretend it smells nice. When I grow up I shan't get married, I've fully made up my mind about that. There is no peace in the house now, and Janet and Georgina squabble with Mabel (the baby's nurse) and grumble about having to do this that and tother for the nursery, and it makes me want to be sick on the spot. Jesus said, "little children, love one another," but I reckon grown-ups don't do much in the way of loving one another, they don't indeed . . . . I said to Mildred to-day, "If babies come out of women's insides, how do they get put there to start with?" And she wouldn't tell me, because she said I wasn't old enough. But if you ask me, I don't believe she knows herself. Mr. Wilcox called to-day and went and had a talk with mamma in bed. He brought her a lovely bunch of grapes, and me some sweets. The baby is going to be called Gladys, and the Vicar is going to christen her, and Mr. Wilcox will be there too. After the christening they are coming back for a glass of shampain, which he told me is called wetting the baby's head. So I said, "Do you pour the shampain on the baby?" And he said, " No, we pour it down our throats instead. Papa says shampain is very expensive, so what a waste it would have been if they were only going to chuck it over the baby. And, dear me, how it does squawk. Mildred says if babies cry an awful lot they sometimes get ruptured, but seeing as she wouldn't tell me what rupture means I looked it up in the dic. and it said the act of breaking or bursting. My word! wouldn't poor mamma be upset if after all that trouble the baby went and burst . . . . Oh, I forgot to say Mr. Wilcox is to be its godfather, and Cousin Agnes its godmother, before she gets married.

Feb. 18.

This morning I found out something so queer it gave me quite a turn, and you could have knocked me over with nothing. Mr. Patmore brought that letter I wrote him at Harrogate to show me some spelling mistakes and wrong grammar, though on the whole he said it was very nice. He said he was very amused about the little gnome I had pretended to see in the old tree. " Pretended!" said I, " I didn't pretend, I really did see him, like I saw him when I was at Auntie's before." Then Mr. Patmore looked rather serious, and said, " Are you a truthful little boy?' And I said I was very truthful about those sort of things, and never made them up. And he said, " Don't you think perhaps you may have a very vivid imagination?" And I said I was quite sure it wasn't my fancy. " Well, well, well," he

77

said, still serious, " we shall have to look into this later," and we went on with our lessons. But that wasn't the end of it. To-day we had geography just before Janet turned up with the milk and biscuits, and we'd been looking at the map of Canada, and Mr. Patmore told me he'd been there once. I don't know why, but I was in one of my knowing moods this morning, so while he was drinking his milk I said, " You won't be cross if I tell you something?" And he promised he wouldn't. So I said, " When you were on that big boat going to Canada, you got sweet on a young lady, didn't you? and thought you'd like her for your Mrs. But after you got to Canada and you didn't see her for a bit, when you *did* see her again, you got sort of disappointed, and thought you wouldn't fancy her as your Mrs. after all. And Mr. Patmore looked mighty surprised and said, " Well, I'm jiggered. How the Dickens did you know that? I'd almost forgotten about it myself." So I said I didn't know how I knew, but that it just comes to me. And he seemed as if he couldn't get over it, and said, " Well, that's most extraordinary. I've never believed in second sight, but I think you must have it. Can you tell me any more?" And I was just going to say no, when I saw (the spirit of) a rum looking man in a great big hat, and he said, " Ask him if he remembers Sam North, and the scrape we got into that day." So I asked him, and he seemed still more surprised, and said, " Don't I remember him indeed. He was one of the best fellows I ever met, and what's more, he saved my life that day." " Well," I said, " there he is now. Can't you see him?" " Go on with you," he said, half laughing, " of course I can't see him. I only wish I could." This seemed to

78

please Mr. Sam North so much that he pulled a jolly face, and said, " Tell him he'll see me all right when he gets over here." Drat it all, I have to go to bed.

Feb. 19.

I had to stop in the middle (of what I was writing) because mamma sent for me to say good-night. So now I will go on. After I told Mr. Patmore about all this, he was more surprised than ever, and said he was jiggered again. When Mr. P. is surprised he always says he is jiggered or blowed. Then he said I was an extraordinary lad, and he didn't know what to make of it all, because he really couldn't see how I could have known about that lady on the boat and about the man in the big (cowboy) hat I saw. So after that, I thought I'd say, " Well, will you now believe about that little gnome, and that I wasn't making it all up?" And he said he certainly didn't think I was telling a lie, though he wondered if it couldn't be explained in some other way. Then he promised he'd tell me the story about the day he nearly lost his life out yonder in Canada ; and he did so at milk and biscuits to-day, and it was ever so exciting . . . . Froyline came this afternoon, and I had my music lesson. I am now allowed to play very little pieces . . . . The Vicar called, and went up to see mamma in bed. He left her a bunch of flowers, and I reckon she was much moved. (Evidently, through having been ordered to go to bed while I was in the midst of writing my diary, I omitted the most important item. Having begun the previous entry by implying that I had made a most momentous discovery, I then quite forgot to mention what the discovery was—I had at length found out, indirectly through my tutor and the incident above related, that my faculties were peculiar to myself, or at least, were not possessed by everyone. This becomes apparent later. Incidentally Mr. Patmore was sufficiently impressed by my sensings to set about studying the claims of Spiritualism, and in the end became quite a convinced spiritualist, though at the time, I myself had never even heard of the cult or its phenomena.)

Date Missing.

Mamma looks herself again, and isn't fat any more in her middle like the Vicar. I suppose it was the baby after all, and that talk about the doctors bringing babies in their bags is all flap-doodle. Somehow I knew it was, deep inside myself. But just for fun I thought I'd ask Froyline to-day how babies arrive. And she laughed a bit uncomfy, and said the storks bring them. But when I asked where the storks got them from, she said, " Perhaps they fly up to God and fetch them down from heaven." So I said I hadn't seen any storks in these parts, and that rather stumped her. But then she said, after a minute, " Oh, but they come at night, so you wouldn't see them." At which I laughed, and said, " You can't humbug *me*." And she laughed too, wiggled her finger at me and said " Little boy, you know too much."

March 21.

Papa says to-day is the first day of Spring, and a lovely day it has been too, all sunny and warm. 'Pon my word! It's fine to wake up and hear the birds singing like mad, and the cocks crowing in Smith's yard, and the hen clucking, and to see the buds on the trees getting all fat and sticky as if they'd been painted with varnish. Mamma said that as March came in like a lion, perhaps now it has started to go out like a lamb . . . I can't think what's come over Janet — at least, I can think, because I have the feeling that she's in love. And her lights are different too, they have gone more pink. But I won't tease her, because I hate being teased when I am in love, though I must say, I'm not very much in love just now. It's a rum thing, but when I've been in love, I wake up one fine day, and somehow, suddenly I'm not in love any more. It's really very bewildering. Now I'm sure Mildred isn't like that, because I could bet she's still gone on her curate with his face like a horse. A queer taste she has, but perhaps it's because she sort of feels sorry for him. You see, papa says he looks as if he hasn't much backbone . . . . Mamma's old bosom friend, Mrs. Chambers, came over from York to-day for dinner, and she has asked me to go and stay with her over Easter, so I am to go after I break up with Mr. Patmore. There's something funny about Mrs. Chamber's face. It usen't to be like that. At first I couldn't make it out, then I saw it was her eyes. She's got eye-lashes on the top lids all right but she's got none on her bottom. A nice thing it would be if she's going to take after Mr. Chambers who hasn't got eye-brows or anything, and has to wear a wig. Mildred says it's an illness.

Good Friday.

I got here on Wednesday, and mamma brought me

81

herself. While she was packing my trunk with all my best things, she said, " Now whatever you do, don't pass any personal remarks." "You mean about Mr. Chamberses' wig?" I said. "About anything," she replied. "You must be on your best behaviour all the time, Mrs. Chambers is very particular. And mind you're attentive in church." So I had to promise of course. "Why haven't the Chamberses got any children," I asked, "Is Mrs. Chambers barren, like some of those women in the Bible?" And mamma wanted to be cross, but got to laughing instead; though she told me I really mustn't use words I didn't understand. "But it's in the Bible," said I. "Never mind," she said, "there are a lot of things in the Bible you are too young to understand."
. . . . I hate Good Fridays. It is awful to think that Jesus had to be crucified because people were so wicked, and I hated the sermon to-day because the clergyman moved me so in church. The Chamberses are very religious, and Mr. reads out prayers in the mornings after breakfast, and the servants and the butler all come in and kneel down on the floor. And yesterday in the middle I wanted to leave the room, but couldn't of course, which made it very awkward. There isn't much to do here, so I read a lot of books. After dinner to-day, Mr. and Mrs. Chambers went to sleep in their chairs, and she snored so loud that she kept waking herself up with her own noise, and then she tried to look as if she hadn't been to sleep at all, but off she went again. I wonder why people do as if they thought it was very wrong to go to sleep, and try to pretend they've been doing no such thing? I can't see as they've any call to be ashamed of themselves. Some people *are* funny. A

82

Mrs. Thomas came to tea yesterday, and spoke so queer I wanted to giggle. Mr. Chambers is her lawyer, and says she's French, though she got married to a Mr. Thomas, who is English. She drops all her h's and leaves out all her s's like people do in France—at least, so Mr. C. says. She kept calling him Mr. Chamber, which sounded very rude, and I was hard put to it not to laugh. (I suppose she thought the s was silent like the t in *pot de chambre!*). The Chamberses have got a dear little dog, and we romp together in the garden. But Mrs. Chambers does talk silly to it, I must say. She calls it my little petty-wetty, and asks it if it is ready for its little dinny-winnys, and whether it wants to go out for a walky-walky, and all the rest of it. Mr. Chambers is nearly as bad. I suppose he has learnt it from Mrs. Chambers. I wish we had a dog, but papa says no. I should like to have about 20 dogs of all sorts and sizes. Perhaps I will when I'm grown up and get a house of my own. I'll keep dogs instead of a wife, and have puppies instead of children. We had hot cross buns for tea, and Mr. Chambers recited:

> Hot cross buns,
> Hot cross buns,
> If you have no daughters
> Give them to your sons.

Easter Sunday.

We went to church in the Cathedral to-day, and the music and singing was lovely. The bishop preached. He looked like a great big babby in his funny sleeves and all. Why ever do clergymen wear things that make you think of nightgowns and little babys? Can it be

that if they think they look like children they reckon
they'll get to heaven the easier because Jesus said, suffer
little children to come unto me, for of such is the kingdom of heaven? But somehow I don't think it's that.
No, there must be some other reason. While I sat in
the cathedral this morning I was wondering about a lot
of things to do with God, even though mamma would
say it was very wicked, because she is always telling
us it's wrong to question what we are told. Then suddenly I saw Jesus, and he said, 'It is never a sin to
think, my son, but it is not always wise to tell one's
thoughts to others." And he smiled that lovely smile
of his, and was gone. So now I've been thinking all the
more, because if Jesus says it isn't wicked to think, I
don't mind what any body else says. Of course I know
mamma is very good and kind and all, but she's not as
clever as Shakespear and can't know everything. What
I should like to know is, if God made the world and
every bit of everything, why did he make a Devil as well
to go about tempting people to be wicked. Seems to me
it 'ud have been much better have left the devil out when
God started to make things. There was a children's
service this afternoon at that church the Chambers
usually go to, and so I went with Annie who is one of
the servants. The parson preached about missionaries
and the heathens and asked us to give our pocket money
so as they could be taught about Christ and then
wouldn't have to go to hell. He said there are millions
of them in places like India, and if we didn't save up
our pennies to put in the missionary box there wouldn't
be enough missionaries to go round. But I do think

it's hard lines that God should make all those millions of heathens who don't ever get a chance.

Easter Monday.

Mamma (had) told Mrs. Chambers I could be trusted out by myself, so this morning I went into the cathedral when there was nothing going on but a few people walking about to see the sights. After I had walked about a bit myself, I felt tired, and sat down in a pew behind a pillow (pillar) where it was quiet and nice. Then I got to thinking about those poor black people again, and what the man who preached yesterday told us about the missionaries, and how sometimes they went to cannibals who eat them up. And I thought it wasn't at all fair that missionaries should have to go and be eaten up because God had made a lot of black men who didn't know about Jesus Christ. Then all at once I saw Jesus, and heard him say: " Be not troubled, my son, for that which the multitudes believe to be true is only the faintest shadow of Truth, and much of it is not the Truth at all. In the Bible is written, Ask and ye shall receive, knock and it shall be opened unto you. But people have received from those who have not asked, and because of this, only very little of the Truth is in them. Ponder on this, and understanding will come."

Then He told me I mustn't tell any one about seeing him and what he'd said, but I could write it down if I wanted to. After that he gave me a blessing and went away. (Needless to add, I had heard all this clairaudiently). Mamma and Mildred are coming to take me back home on Wednesday. I shall be sorry to go, because I like York. I like places that feel old.

Arnold and Henry and I were allowed to take sandwitches to-day and go for a long walk to the woods to pick bluebells. It was lovely and I saw a lot of little mannikins doing something to the leaves of a huge old beech tree, though I couldn't make out what they were really up to. They look very old fashioned and wear funny clothes like people used to wear long ago. They were always smiling and seemed to have great fun. I saw a lot of little elves too. I told Arnold about them when Henry was busy picking somewhere else. He said he couldn't see them, but he had the decency not to jeer at me, so I don't mind telling Arnold things, though of course I mustn't tell him about Jesus. But I didn't tell Henry, because I thought he might say something to his father (the Vicar) about it, and then *he* might go and sneak to mamma . . . There is a nice little gurgling stream which runs through the wood, and we paddled in it, and Henry and Arnold splashed each other and got their clothes all wet. Henry can pull awful faces. He said one day his papa caught him at it, and told him if he wasn't careful he might stick like that. But he said, " Of course I didn't believe him." Henry is very clever at belching too, just for fun, and did some fine ones for us. But once he overdid it a bit and was nearly sick. He says the Vicar sometimes belches after dinner, and then sort of does as if it had only been a cough. Arnold can stand on his head. I tried too, but didn't meet with much success. Henry did it against a tree, and then fell over in a lot of prickles, which was rather mortifying. After we had eaten our sandwitches and picked some more bluebells, we walked home again and got back in time for tea. Mamma asked me afterwards if Henry had had anything to say about the Vicar. So seeing as I couldn't blab about the belching, or she might have been cross, I told her Henry had said he had indigestion sometimes after his dinner. I thought that would do all right, because belching *is* supposed to come from indigestion, so why not?

May 1.

I was asked to Charlie Baine's to tea this afternoon. I can't say as he's got any thinner since I used to sit next to him under Miss Enid. He still goes there, and I asked him how he could go on stomaching her awful waxes. But he's a queer chap is Charlie and said her waxes didn't make much odds to him. I think he is so fat he doesn't much mind about anything save birds' eggs. Miss Enid used to call him Mr. Lazy Lump when she wanted to be nasty, which I thought was going too far, because if he is a lump, he can't help being as he's made. After tea he pulled out his eggs. Some of them are ever so pretty, but I couldn't help saying I think it's a cruel mean trick to go and take the eggs away from the poor little birds after they'd made their nests and all, and are so happy. But he wasn't of the same mind, and it was no use talking. When one says anything to Charlie, he justs looks at one like a cow, only he hasn't got such beautiful eyes as some cows I've met with. Mamma is frightened of cows. When we were at the Lakes she went and hid behind a gate. I suppose she thinks they are going to butt at her or something. Charlie has a book of ghost stories. He asked me if I believe in ghosts? And I said, yes. Then he wanted to know if I'd ever seen one, and I said, lots. "Honour bright?" said he. "Honour bright," said I. "Well, I never," said he. "Weren't you afraid?" "Not when they're nice ghosts," said I, "but I don't like nasty ones." "The servants say this house is haunted," said he, "but pater says it's all rubbish, and flies into a rage when we talk about it. The slavies make out they can hear somebody going up the stairs, but they can't see the thing." "I reckon they're quite right," said I, "I saw it myself. It's a young woman. She has a dress which sticks out all round, and sort of makes a noise; but you mustn't tell anyone, because I may get into a row." "I say!" said Charlie, "do you really mean that, or are you fooling?" "Honour bright," said I. "Upon my Sam, you make me feel all funny," said he. "Go on," said I, "she won't hurt you. She's quite a respectable kind of ghost, and means no harm." After that it was time for me to go home.

May 8.

The baby was christened to-day, and kicked up an awful shindy when the Vicar wet it. Cousin Agnes came to be its Godmother and is staying till Monday. I'm so glad. She is going to be married in July and Mildred is to be dressed up as one of the bridesmaids. Mamma says Cousin Agnes looks radiant, and I must say her lights look very pink; I reckon it's because she's so in love. I've somehow seen that when people are in love their lights go pinker. After she's married, her name will be Mrs. Fred Hopkins, which seems a pity, because Hopkins isn't much of a name when you come to think of it, though Mamma says he is a most gentlemanly young man, judging from his likeness. He is going to come and fetch her back to Ilkly on Monday, so then we shall get to know him, and be able to see for ourselves. After the christening, the Vicar and Mr. Wilcox and the others came back to our house and they each had a glass of that shampain which papa got out to wet the baby's head. It was full of bubbles, and the Vicar belched once, and pretended it was a cough; but *I* knew better. Mildred was on her best behaviour, and all shy, because Mr. Amery, her sweetheart, was there too. I still can't think what she sees in him, but you never can tell. The Vicar patted me on the head, and told me what a big man I was getting. How silly! I know that I'm not anywhere near getting a big man, so why pretend all that? I suppose he thought I'd be pleased. Well, I wasn't, so he might as well have held his tongue. The baby isn't quite as ugly as it was, but that isn't saying much.

May 19.

Ever since the time I told Mr. Patmore that thing about the lady on the boat and the man in the rum hat, he seems to like to ask me all sorts of questions over our milks. He wants to know what other things I've seen and all. He told me he'd been reading about something called—and he said a long word beginning with spirit (Spiritualism)—but he couldn't tell me all about it, because he thought my mother would be shocked. So I asked if it was rude. And he laughed and said it wasn't a bit rude, but some people thought it was wicked. Then he asked me what my mother thought about me seeing things, and said he supposed she knew? And I told him I daren't tell her any more, because she got angry and made out I was telling fibs. And he said, " Ah, hah, that's what I thought." After that he told me lots of clever men believed in ghosts, and that Shakespear stuck them into his plays, as I knew; but till he'd met me he'd thought them all fancy, and rather wished Shakespear had left them out. On Saturday he is going to fetch me and take me to have tea with his Mrs., as he says she'd like to see me. Then he's going to bring me home again. I'm wondering what his Mrs. will look like. It will be great fun. I feel as if Mr. Patmore was my chum as well as my teacher, and it's fine. When I think of Miss Enid—Golly! Poor papa has got lumbaygo and walks about all double like an old gentleman. Mildred laughs behind his back and says he *does* look funny. So he does, but it's a bit hard lines, because mamma says it hurts like anything.

Sunday, May 23.

It is an awful bother that mamma said I was only to put down about sacred things on Sundays, because I wanted to write about my tea party at Mr. Patmore's yesterday, and now I shall have to wait till to-morrow. I do wish mamma wasn't so particular. Mildred was reading a novel to-day, and mother caught her at it, and said it was very wicked to read novels on a Sunday, and took it from her. But I know papa reads novels on the Sabbath because I've seen him do it. Went to Sunday school this afternoon. I don't much like Sunday school, such a lot of poor children come, and they do smell so nasty. Sometimes the Vicar turns up at the end and plays a hymn. I think he rather fancies himself on the harmonium, but he seems to play an awful lot of wrong notes. Froyline would think it simply appalling if she heard him, and would pull ghastly faces. She would that. Oh, I forgot; Mr. Patmore says I'm not to use that expression. He says it's all right for people like Hobbs (the gardener) but it doesn't sound nice for *me* to be saying it. Well, I won't do it again.

May 24.

To-day not being Sunday any more I can put down about the tea party on Saturday. Mr. Patmore's Mrs. reminds me a bit of that Mrs. Bird who mamma calls such a nice unassuming little body. She is very small for a grown-up, but ever so pleasant and kind, and I liked her lights. They live in a terrace right the other side of the town and their house isn't nearly as big as ours, but very cosy. We had a grand tea. Hot buttered currant buns and lots of jam, and little cakes all covered over with sugar. Mrs. Patmore was very pressing and told me to eat as much as ever I could. There was no body else there but me. When Mr. Patmore was sitting in his armchair after tea and smoking his pipe, which smelt very nice, I saw a big black dog sitting at his feet. So I said, " Did you ever have a big black dog?" And they both looked sad, and told me they used to have one called Jock, but that he died last Autumn, and wondered why I had asked. So I told them I saw it sitting by the chair, and it knew we were talking about it because it was wagging its tail. And that seemed to surprise and please them both very much. Mrs. Patmore said Mr. P. had told her I was such a clever little boy and had second sight, which made me feel a bit shy, because it was like as if she'd said I was a clever little boy because I could see without spectacles. But somehow I couldn't tell her that, so I just said it was very kind of her to say so. Mamma says one must always do that when a person says something special nice, and I think it's quite a good plan. Mr. Patmore said he had always thought animals ought to have souls, but most persons believed they hadn't. So he was a lot cheered up when I told him I had seen his dog, and so was his Mrs. I wonder why the P's should think it fine when I tell them I see things, and mamma only gets waxy and thinks it's wicked? Really it's all very bewildering, I must say. Before I had to go home, I saw a man who said he was Mrs. P's papa, though he didn't seem at all old. When she asked me what he looked like, I told her his face was a bit queer because he had sticking-out teeth. And she was a lot surprised, and said it was quite right, because her papa's teeth did stick out rather, and that he'd died when she was only ten years old. He (the spirit) told me to tell them that he was often here, though they couldn't see him, and he was very glad I had come to-day because I could give them a message. He said he wanted them to persevere with —the long word starting with spirit (Spiritualism), as it 'ud make all the difference (to their lives), and that the spirits were very pleased about it, and had known for a long time that I could see things. He said some more, but I can't remember it properly. At all events the P's were very pleased, and I enjoyed myself very much and was sorry when it was time to go home. I do think it is ripping to be able to make people feel sort of happy. But I did wish afterwards I hadn't eaten so may of those cakes and things, I got a bit of belly-ake. As soon as Mr. Patmore had seen me home, mamma came out, and after she'd thanked him for all his kindness, said she hoped I had been a good boy. And he told her I had been the perfect little gentleman. But Lawks! if she only knew what I'd been up to. Ah well, if she *will* be so particular, that's *her* look out.

June 7.

Janet has given notice. I knew there was something up because her lights have been looking different, a bit like Cousin Agnes'es. And now if she isn't going to leave us all and get married to Mr. Thingumibob, the confectioner. I shall miss her something awful but perhaps it won't be so very bad because she won't be far off, and I dare say I can see her when I go there to buy a pennorth of sweets. Mamma is very put out, because Janet has been with us so long, and she'll have to try and meet with another servant who may not be half so nice.

June 15.

Mr. Patmore has found out that the lights I see round people is called an aura, and he told me how to spell it too. We talked a lot about auras to-day over milk, and it seemed to please him very much, because he asked a crowd of questions. I told him some peoples' (auras) were just a sort of dirty mess and nothing but a horrid muddle, but other people had nice auras with a lot of lovely bright colours. Then there were people whose auras ended all of a sudden, (i.e. they had a hard outline) like mamma's, and others that got thinner and thinner at the edge like a (melting) cloud. (I later on discovered that the type of aura I then described as "a dirty mess" denoted a complete lack of emotional control, with little or no mentality, and that an aura with a hard outline was a sign of conventionality.). I told Mr. Patmore that his aura was very pretty, with yellow and some pink and a little green and blue, and he was very delighted.

July 9.

We have been to Ilkley for Cousin Agnes' wedding, and got back last night. We stayed at a hotel. I was allowed to go as a great treat. Mamma had a new dress on and looked very spry. Every body got excited, and there was a grand meal after the wedding with an enormous cake all covered with white sugar. I thought it looked nicer than it tasted, which was disappointing. Aunt Susan blubbed at the wedding, though I don't know why. Mamma says ladies often blub when their daughters get married, because it is like losing them. Cousin Agnes had to promise to love, honour and obey Mr. Hopkins, which I thought a bit much, I must say. A nice thing if Mr. Hopkins turned out to be very wicked and ordered her to bag some one's purse, then she'd have to obey him. I wonder who made up the marriage service? I'm sure it wasn't God or Jesus. Mildred thought no end of herself in her grand get-up as bridesmaid, but she behaved pretty well for *her*. I reckon Cousin Agnes felt jolly shy when she had to go to bed with Mr. Hopkins last night. They went to London for their honeymoon. Mr. H. has quite a nice aura and I get the feeling that they'll be happy, (which

94

proved to be correct), but somehow I don't think they'll live to be old. (Also correct). They are going to take a house near Manchester, where Mr. H. has his business. It's a rum thing, but I've got the notion that some people have sort of known each other before, and then meet again and love each other. But I can't quite make it out . . . . I had just written this down when all at once I saw Jesus; and he said: " You are right, my son, and have divined a hidden truth about which one day you will have understanding." And then he smiled, and was gone. I wish he would stay longer. The weather is that hot all my clothes are sticking to me. Mamma feels the heat something awful and does nothing but sigh all the time. Mildred pretends she likes it, just to be contrary. The butter we had for tea had all gone soft. Papa says he thinks we are going to have a thunderstorm. I shouldn't be surprised. Georgina declares that her corns hurt her and that's a sure sign of rain, and Janet says the cat washed behind its ears, and that's a sure sign too. Ah well, we shall see.

July 10.

We did have a thunderstorm. It was in the night, and a fine row it made. I hated the noise and couldn't sleep, so I got out of bed and looked at it through the window. But the things (nature spirits) I saw in the clouds were so wicked looking that I went back to bed and hid under the bed clothes. Papa came into my room to see if I was in a funk after there had been an enormous clap, which was very decent of him. Georgina says a thunderstorm is God being angry with wicked people, or something of the sort, but papa says that's

95

all nonsense. Anyhow it is much cooler to-day, and I am mighty thankful, and so is mamma. Arnold came to tea, which we had in the summerhouse. When Janet brought out the tray he was standing on his head in the middle of the lawn, and then he walked on his hands, which she thought very clever, and asked him if he was going to be an acrobat when he grew up.

July 12.

I do think Charlie Baines is mean. He went and sneaked on me, and I got into a row to-day. Mamma said she'd heard in a roundabout way that I'd said the Baines's house was haunted, and I'd seen something, and that Mr. Baines had been very anoyed, and said he wouldn't let Charlie ask me there again. Mamma was in an awful wax, because she said she thought I'd got over all that nonsense, as she called it, and she really didn't know what she was going to do with me. After she'd gone on at me for an awful long time, she said she'd decided to tell Mr. Patmore to set me a lot of lines to write out like they do at schools. But though I felt horrid, I couldn't help laughing a bit inside myself, because Mr. Patmore will be on my side, and I wonder what he'll have to say about it?

July 13.

When we were having lessons this morning in the summerhouse, mamma turned up looking very serious, and told Mr. Patmore I had been a very naughty un-truthful little boy and had made mischief, and I ought to be punished. So Mr. Patmore looked shocked and said he was very sorry to hear it, though I knew he wasn't shocked really, because I had told him before what to expect. Anyhow, mamma said I ought to be given those lines to write out or something nasty to do, and Mr. Patmore had to tell her he'd have a serious talk to me about it, and then decide what ought to be done. After which intermation mamma cleared out. When she'd gone, Mr. Patmore pulled a funny face, a bit like Henry can do, and said, " And now what?" I do love Mr. P. more and more. But he told me he'd have to do something so as to get even (put himself right) with mamma. He wasn't cross, but he said it was silly of me to go and tell schoolboys like that young ass Charlie about what I saw, because they only went and blabbed and got me into trouble, and if he were me, he'd be very careful who I told things to in the future. Then he said he really couldn't punish me for telling lies, because I hadn't told any lies. But if he didn't set me something to write out to please mamma, she might give him the sack, and that would be a fine todo. Well, the long and short of it is, he asked me what rather long piece of poetry I'd like to get by heart, because if I was made to write it out three times, I'd know it by then. And I thought this such a fine idea that I chose Gray's Elegy; and that was the end of that. We break up on the 23rd, but I can't say as I particularly want to, I shall hate saying good-bye to Mr. Patmore.

July 20.

I saw grandpa to-day, and he told me they (the spirits) had got papa to find Mr. Patmore for my tutor, and that they were very pleased with the way I was getting on. Grandpa said heaven isn't a bit like what

97

people think, and it's much nicer. He told me that by and by crowds of people will believe in the spirits, something like they believe in Jesus now, and they'll all be much happier and won't mind such a lot about death. I asked him (formulated the question mentally) if people stayed old in heaven when they had died old? And he laughed and said, no. He told me that where he was, people could make themselves look just as they wanted to look. If they like to think of themselves looking young, they look young, and the other way round too. He says he makes himself look old when he comes to see me, because if he didn't I wouldn't be able to know (recognise) him. Though Arnold doesn't jeer at me for seeing things, he said one day, if ghosts are supposed to be the spirits of dead people, why do they have clothes on, because clothes can't have spirits? So I thought I'd ask Grandpa why he wasn't naked, or why all spirits aren't naked. And this seemed to tickle him a lot. But I couldn't catch him out, he is too sharp. He said, " Do *you* think of yourself as going about naked?" So I said, " No, I didn't." Then he said, " Well, neither do we. I have just told you, my lad, that we look (appear) as we think of ourselves. That is why people over here wear such a lot of different sorts of clothes, and why even I wear clothes that aren't the fashion any more with you in your world. But you must not tell your mother about all this," he said, " or she will be shocked. Your mother is a good woman, but it is given to you to know many things which she doesn't know. But take care, my lad, that you don't get proud on that account, because there are many things that she knows which you don't know." After that he went away.

98

July 21.

I had my last music lesson (before the holidays) with Fräulein (correctly spelt at last) yesterday. She does talk funny sometimes. She told me she went a picnic all by herself the other day, which I thought couldn't have been much fun. She said, "whenever I go somewhere I take a cold sossage and some bread and fruit." So when I laughed, she wanted to know what I was laughing at. And I had to tell her that to go somewhere means to want to leave the room, at which she was mighty surprised, and laughed and said, "Your English language makes me quite mad." Then she said something about spelling which I hadn't thought of before, but reckoned it would be a joke to catch Mr. P. over. What I'd like to know is who made up spelling, cause he must have been an awful jackass, and a fibber too. When we did grammar one day, I remember Mr. P. saying there were only five vowels. But the dic. says a vowel is a sound uttered by simply opening the mouth, so that's a fib. I reckon there are eleven vowels, and I told Mr. P. so to-day. "How do you make that out?" said he. "Well, here goes," said I, and produced out "ah, aw, a, e, eh, i, o, oo, ow, oy, u." "Hum," said Mr. Patmore, "I hadn't thought of that, but all those sounds are in our language, as you say. Very smart. What else have you been up to?" Fräulein wants to know," said I, " why o-f-f spells off, but c-o-u-g-h spells coff, and n-o-w spells now, but p-l-o-u-g-h spells plow, and t-r-u-e spells true, but t-h-r-o-u-g-h spells thrue, and why c-u-f-f spells cuff, but e-n-o-u-gh spells enuff?" "God knows," said Mr. Patmore, "and *He* won't tell. It's all very silly. But you ask Fräulein with *my* compliments, why in *her* language a girl is newter? That's just as silly." Mamma told us today that Mr. Wilcox has to leave his rooms, because he has found out that Mrs. Tims (his landlady) is a wicked old thing and took advantage of him.

July 23.

A huge surprise to-day. I am to go for my holiday with Mr. and Mrs. Patmore to a place called Harlech in Wales. What fun. We are going early in August. Mildred has been asked to go and stay with that school chum of her's, Ethel Mckay, and mamma and papa and the baby are going to Buxton, because papa says he has reumatism and wants to go and drink the waters. I wonder what mamma and Mr. Patmore were up to, they were closeted together twice after my lessons, and Mr. P. told me this morning it was all about my going away with him and his Mrs. Papa said he didn't want me to be weeks without doing any lessons at all, so when I am away we are going to do just an hour's lessons a day except on Saturdays, and I shan't mind that a bit. I was jolly glad about it all, because I didn't have to say good-bye to Mr. P. for so long now, as we are off in a fortnight. Besides I love being with Mr. Patmore, and like his Mrs. too. Perhaps Henry is to be asked for a week, though mamma isn't sure yet. It depends on what the Vicar says. I hope he comes, though I am a bit glad he won't be there all the time, because I like seeing things (clairvoyantly) for Mr. and Mrs. Patmore, and I have to shut up when Henry's there, else he'd think me dotty. Janet is going to be married while we are away, and is bunking with her Mr. to Blackpool for their honeymoon. Georgina is going somewhere for her holidays, and old Mrs. Prettyman is coming to take care of the house and the cat and the parrot. I shan't be at all sorry to get away from the baby for a bit, it does squawk such a lot and vexes me when I'm trying to do my lessons for Mr. P. If mamma went and produced out any more babies it would be appalling, and anyhow I'd much sooner have had a little brother. Of course I should hate the baby to get ill or die or anything, but I do wish it would give over making such a blithering row.

July 29.

A funny thing happened this afternoon. Auntie Maud came over for the day and brought her old mother who is 83. Before they turned up I asked mamma, " If Aunt Maud is your sister-in-law, then is Mrs. Kidd your mother-in-law and my grand mother-in-law or is she your aunt-in-law and my great aunt-in-law?" But Mamma only laughed, and didn't seem to know, or didn't want to bother her head. " You'd better ask your father," she said. Anyhow she told us (my sister and myself) the old geazer had lost her memory, and if she talked funny we must be sure and not laugh. But of course that made us want to laugh all the more, and Mildred said to me afterwards she nearly wet hei drawers. There's something very rum with the old thing's aura, it is just a dirty mess like some kids I've set eyes on and somehow I got a feeling as if she hadn't got a soul. (6) I can't make it out. While we were in the morning-room waiting for dinner, she said, quite cross, " When are we going to have

breakfast?" " But you've had your breakfast, dear," said
Auntie Maud, all sweet, "we're just going to have
dinner." Then when Janet came into say dinner was
ready, she said to Aunt Maud, " You've got a new ser-
vent, I haven't seen her before." So Auntie Maud had
to tell her they weren't in Harrogate but had come to
see mamma for the day. I was jolly glad when we'd
finished dinner and I was allowed to clear off. But the
worst thing happened afterwards. I came in from the
garden to go to the closet, and when I opened the door,
I'm jiggered if the old girl wasn't sitting on the seat.
"Would you!" she said, and shook her fist at me. It
gave me quite a turn, though Mildred and I had a good
laugh together afterwards. Mildred got a prize at
school.

Aug. 7.

We are now at Harlech, and got here yesterday in
the pouring wet. It was an awful long journey, but
there were lovely things to see out of the window, and
I liked being with Mr. and Mrs. Patmore who are so
kind. Harlech is on a hill with a huge old castle. It is
only a small place, but we came here because the P's
knew of some nice rooms where we should be well seen
to—at least that's what they told mamma. It has rained
ever since we got here, which is very mortifying, but
Mr. Patmore is going to teach me how to play chess,
because he says it's the finest indoor game in the world.
The people here talk as if they were half singing, and
sometimes I can't make out what they are wanting to
say. Mrs. P. knits a lot. This place has such a different
feel to home. I'm sure I shall see no end of fairies and

gnomes and all that, but I do wish it would give over raining, else we'll be stuck in the house and I shall see nothing whatever.

Aug. 12.

Grandpa turned up to-day after tea, and when I told the P's he was in the room they seemed very pleased and wanted to know what he had to say, so I repeated out loud what he said. Grandpa did the polite and bowed, and said to Mr. P. like, " Good day to you, my dear sir," and then to Mrs. P., " Good day to you, my dear madam," and they said good day to him. Then Grandpa said he was very glad we had all come here, as this was a very old part of the world and used to be part of a huge continent called Atlantis or some such name, most of which had gone down under the sea, and that the something or other, I've forgotten the words (probably Nature-forces) were very strong and would help me to see things. Then Mr. P. wanted to know if he could ask some questions. And Grandpa said, " I am at your service." So Mr. P. thought he would get pencil and paper and put down what Grandpa said as I repeated it. First he wanted to know what we looked like to grandpa, and grandpa said we looked just like ghosts. And Mr. P. thought that very funny because we are supposed to be solid, he said. Then grandpa laughed and told Mr. P. he was smoking a pipe, which was quite true. And then he said if Mr. P. was the sultan of somewhere or other, I forget where he said, he would be smoking a thing called a hubblebubble and sucking his smoke through water, and it was something like that. The spirits were like the smoke and we were like the water and they could go right through us and see right through us, because our parts (particles) are really quite far apart, though we don't know it. Grandpa said a lot more, but I can't remember it by heart. He said he'd come again to-morrow and tell us some other things if we liked.

Aug. 13

This afternoon we all went and had a squint at Harlech castle, and I was able to tell Mr. and Mrs. P. what it looked like before it was all in pieces, and about the furniture and all. (7) And the P's were very surprised and wondered how I did it. Perhaps they thought I was making it all up, but I wasn't. Grandpa came again after tea and stayed so long that it's now my bedtime and I can't write down what he said, so will have to do it by and bye.

Aug. 16.

The weather has been too scrumptious to go sitting in doors and writing my diary, but to-day it's pouring again like billyo, so I shall try and write down what grandpa said. Mr. Patmore asked me if I put everything in my diary about him and grandpa coming to see us and all. And when I told him I did, he pulled a face and said he lived on tender hooks for fear the mater might see it one day, and then he'd get into an awful row for encouraging me. But when I told him I was mighty careful to keep it locked up in my special box, and that grandpa (had) said a long time ago he was very pleased I was keeping the diary, he said he would hope for the best. Old grandpa is ever so polite when

he talks to the P's, and is always calling them my dear
sir and my dear madam, which makes me want to laugh.
But I wish he didn't have to use such long words sometimes, because I can't remember them properly when I
want to write them down, which is a blithering nuisance.
I asked him why grandmamma never came to see us too?
And he said something about spirits getting thought-
bound like birds getting egg-bound, and made us all
laugh because it seemed such a funny thing to say. He
told us that while the grandmater was still on earth,
she reckoned, same as a lot of people do, that she and
a few others who thought exactly like she did, were the
only people what were going to be saved. " And now,"
said grandpa, " she lives in a world of thoughts which
she and others have created by their own fallacious convictions. In our Father's house are many mansions."
I got this out of Mr. P. who had written it down. And
he has helped me with the next bit too. When we asked
Grandpa what about *him?* He said, though he (had)
believed in God and all that, he'd never made up his
mind too much what the other world was going to be
like, so now he didn't spend his life singing hymns round
an imaginary throne of God like grandma does. Grandpa
doesn't mind saying naughty things. He told us grandma had been an obstinate old woman, and she was still
obstinate now, and nothing he could say was going to
change her (outlook) till she got sick of it and began
looking round for something better. He told us it was
a great mistake to have preconceived notions like my late
lamented grandmother; but seeing as I didn't quite know
what he meant, I asked Mr. Patmore, who says it's if
people are too cock sure of a thing when they've nothing

proper to go on. I'm tired now and want to leave off. *Aug. 17.*

Another beastly wet day, and I've no news, so I'm going to put down some more of what grandpa said, with Mr. P's help. Grandpa told us that some parsons talk an awful lot of stuff and nonsense about the next world, and pretend we shall all go to sleep till the day of resurrection. And so crowds of people (spirits) when they get over there and find themselves alive and kicking, can't believe they are dead, and it's no end of a job to convince them that they've shuffled off their old bodies. Same with people what didn't believe anything at all and are agnostics and believe we have all come out of monkeys. I once heard the mater talking about agnostics, which Mr. P. has told me how to spell, and she said they were all dreadful wicked people who said there was no God. But grandpa says they aren't wicked but have only got all muddled up and think they know a fine lot because they believe in a think called evolution. Had to ask Mr. P how to spell this long word. Rather funny, Mr. P. told me after grandpa had gone that he used to know an agnostic, who is dead now, and he was the person who told him about our lodgings. I can't be sure, but I've just got the feeling that he may pop round one of these fine days to have a squint at Mr. P. or something. Played at chess this afternoon. Of course Mr. P. always wins, though once he let me have his Queen. But I knew he did it on purpose because he wanted to be nice. He can't diddle *me*. So now he takes off his Queen beforehand, because it makes it harder for him without her. This is called a handy cap, though I can't say why.

Aug. 18.

I had a letter from mamma to-day telling me about Buxton and all. She says there's a lovely band there. I wish I could hear it, though I'd much rather be here with the Patmores except for that. Mamma finishes off by saying she hopes I was attentive at church on Sunday. I shan't tell her we never went at all, and that Mr. P. and I went a walk instead, because he thought we ought to take advantage of the fine weather. Mr. P. says one can worship God in Nature by being thankful for all the beautiful things He has given us, and I am of the same mind to be sure. Mrs. P. went to service by herself. Somehow I think ladies like going to church better than gents. But I suppose I shall have to go next Sunday or there will be a row, if ma asks questions.

Aug. 20.

Last night, just before I was going to sleep, grandpa turned up for a minute, and said if I'd make some excuse to go into the kitchen I'd see something there. This morning Mrs. Evans forgot the butter for breakfast, so I went and asked for it and saw an old geazer (in spirit form) sitting in an armchair by the fire. I'd like to have asked him what he thinks he's about, but I couldn't, because of Mrs. Evans being there .... This afternoon Mr. P. helped me to make a lovely sand castle with a mote. I've fallen in love with a girl we see walking about. I wish I could know her, but I've no excuse. She has the loveliest brown eyes. Sometimes she and a boy I reckon is her brother, play with two balls on the sea shore. She throws one of the balls to him to catch and he throws the other ball to her. They are quite clever at it. If only she would lose one of her balls and I could pick it up and hand it her back. But no such luck. Mrs. Patmore seems to have caught cold and has got the snuffles. Henry is coming next week.

Aug. 24.

Rather funny after grandpa saying about some spirits not knowing they are dead, and me getting that feeling. Yesterday after dinner I saw a man in the room, and we had great fun with him. When I told Mr. Patmore he was there, he said, " Let's ask him what he wants," and he got his pencil ready to put it all down in short hand which he can do a bit. So to-day he gave me what he'd written for dictation lesson to put in my diary. It will be grand when it's all printed like Mr. Pepys, though I shall have to wait till I'm old, because of course mamma would kick up an awful rumpus if she saw it. The spirit who turned up was that old friend of Mr. P's, but not half as nice. The first thing he said was " Hello, Patmore. Fancy seeing you here." Then Mr. P. asked who he was. And he said, " What a question, and that his name was Jimmy Cliff, and he was surprised that Mr. P. didn't recognise him. So Mr. P. was very surprised too, and said he was blowed, but that of course he couldn't recognise him because he couldn't see people who were dead, though I think he said another word. And now I'll write what Mr. P. gave me for dictation, which was quite easy because Mr. Cliff didn't use such long words as grandpa. Mr. Patmore says I can put P. for Patmore and C. for Cliff if I like so as to save time. So that is what I shall do, though it won't look very nice without the misters.

C.—What are you writing there?

P.—I'm writing down what you say.

C.—What the devil for?

P.—Because I want to remember what you tell us.

C.—What nonsense.

P.—Not at all, I'm interested. I'm very pleased you have come. But what gave you the idea?

C.—I like the place, and wanted to see it again. It was I who told you about these rooms.

P.—Yes, I know you did. Tell me, how are you feeling?

C.—I never felt better in my life, physically, but mentally—well, I seem to be a bit confused. It's damn queer.

P.—You used to be an Agnostic. I suppose you've altered your views now?

C.—Of course I haven't. Why should I?

P.—Because you must know there's an after-life now.

C.—I don't know anything of the kind, and don't believe any of the people who tell me all that nonsense. Who is this young lad, by the way, and why does he have to repeat to you everything I say?

P.—Because he can see you and hear you, and I can't.

C.—Have you gone blind and deaf?

P.—Of course not. But you are now a spirit, and I can't see spirits.

C.—I am not a spirit. I don't believe in spirits and never have.

P.—But surely you can't think you are still on this earth? Can't you remember what happened?

C.—I remember feeling infernally ill. Then I lost consciousness and after that I woke up feeling better than ever.

P.—Yes, and then what happened?

C.—Look here, Patmore, I resent all this interrogation and your writing down everything I say like a policeman.

P.—Sorry, my dear Cliff, but I'm very much interested. You don't appear to realise that you are what we down here call dead, though I appreciate the fact that you feel very much more alive.

C.—There's no down here about it. You talk as if I were standing on a cloud and you were below. I never heard such rubbish. The only thing that's the matter with me is that sometimes my sight and my hearing seem a bit queer.

P.—You mean perhaps that we look a bit dim to you and sound rather far off?

C.—Yes, in a sense.

P.—That's because you are a spirit and we have still got physical bodies.

C.—I refuse to believe that I am a spirit. There are no spirits. When we died that is the end of us. You annoy me. You always did annoy me when we got talking on this subject, because you will not face facts. You can't get round science, and science declares that we have evolved from monkeys. I'm going. I've had enough of this futile argument. We shall never convince one another, so what's the good of talking? Good-bye.

When he'd cleared out, Mr. Patmore pulled a funny face and said he hadn't changed a bit and always went

on like that when he was alive. He said Mr. Cliff had
been taken ill in the street and had died in a hospital.
Mrs. P. wasn't there because she felt bilious and went
to her room after dinner. But Mr. P. told her about it
all afterwards and read out what he had written down
What fun it all is to be sure.

Aug. 25.

Henry is here now. We have to sleep in the same
room, which is rather nice because we can talk instead
of going to sleep when we aren't really tired. Mrs. Patmore tells us to be sure and not stay awake talking, but
come to that I don't suppose she minds, she is so very
decent. Henry does funny things to himself in bed, and
wanted to teach me, but I informed him that a little
girl at Birkdale had told me all about that, and he
needn't think he could teach his grandma to suck duck
eggs. This morning he wanted to dig tunnels in the
sandhills, but Mr. P. wouldn't let us, because he says
they might fall in and then we'd get smothered. I can't
write much in my diary while Henry is here, as he always wants to be doing something. He talks of the
Vicar and his Mrs. as the pater and the mater. I have
decided that I shall call papa and mamma that too. I
think papa and mamma sounds so blithering silly, and I
don't much like mother and father either.

Sunday.

Henry told me in bed this morning that he wasn't
going to service unless Mr. Patmore made him. When
he asked Mr. P. at breakfast about it, Mr. P. said he
never believed in forcing any body to go to church if

111

they didn't want to, but what would his father say if he played truant? So Henry said, "I shall go as far as the porch with Mrs. Patmore, and then if the pater asks, I can say I've been to church." This seemed to amuse Mr. Patmore no end, though Mrs. Patmore pretended to be shocked but had to laugh. 'Pon my word, Henry is a rum chap. I reckon Mrs. Patmore thinks I'm a rum chap too. I had to promise the mater I would read a bit of the bible every morning. So to-day I asked at dinner what it means to lust after a woman in one's own heart, and Mrs. P. half laughed and looked as if she didn't know where to look, and Mr. P. turned up his eyes to the ceiling, and then said there were some queer old fashioned words in the bible which he couldn't explain just then. I suppose it was something rude. But when I asked Henry about it afterwards, he said he thought it had something to do with making babies, but he wasn't sure. I wish I knew. I quite forgot I'm not supposed to write in my diary on a sunday. But it's done now, and I'm blowed if I'm going to cross it all out. At all events I did mention the bible, so that's something.

Aug. 30.

When Mrs. P. had gone to the shops and Mr. P. was safely in the closet, where he generally takes the newspaper and stays some time, Henry and I thought we'd look up *lust.* But as we didn't know what the words meant we aren't much further. Why in the name of goodness doesn't the dic. tell us what it means instead of giving a long word which no body can understand and which I've forgotten how to spell? Henry says the dic. is a silly book and he's no patience with it . . . . I had a letter from Fräulein to-day. She says she hopes there is a piano, and that I'll be able to practice diligently a bit. But there is only an old harmonium here, and I can't play it because I can't reach those things at the bottom which make the wind. We went a walk in the hills and saw some lovely sheep in a field with such sad looking faces. It makes me feel awful to think they go and get killed for us to eat with our dinners. Mr. Patmore says there are people called some word like vegitaters who won't eat sheep or cows or anything. That's what I should like to be, only I suppose the mater wouldn't let me. I expect she'd say, like she always does, " What would people think if I was different to any one else?" I wonder why the mater wants every body to be the same as two peas?

Aug. 30.

To-day is that hot I hardly know how to contain myself. Henry says he likes the hot weather, but complains that it makes him stink. I smell a bit sour too, which is most objectionable. Mr. Patmore looks very funny; he declares the sun has caught his nose: at all events it is very red. Henry and Mr. P. bathed this morning and I tried too, but it gave me the pitterpats and I couldn't get my breath and Mr. P. says I mustn't try again as it doesn't suit me. On Thursday Henry is off home—at least he is not really going home yet, because he's been asked to stay somewhere on root. I shall be sorry when he has shunted, because he's such a caution and I like him extremely. The only draw back is that I have to shut up seeing things for

Mr. Patmore and his Mrs. when Henry is here. I asked him for fun what his pater (the Vicar) usually talked about, and he said he usually talked shop. If I told the mater that, I reckon she'd be mighty shocked at him calling the church a shop. But of course I shan't tell her; that would be mean. Henry's big brother is in the army somewhere in India. He says when they have dinner it is called officers' mess which he said reminds him of cows. Then he asked me if I knew what an innuendo was? And I said it was when you hadn't to play the piano so loud. But he jeered at me, and said it was when something polite means something rude. So I asked him how he knew that. And he said his pater often says at meals, " Now then, no innuendoes, please." Saw grandpa for half a jiffy while I was washing my hands, but he didn't stop, and only came to have a squint at us.

Sept. 2.

Henry absconded this morning. Yesterday we caught a man sprawling all over a woman in the sandhills, which I thought very funny. But Henry says when common people want to get married they often do that before-hand. He said even ladies and gents are supposed to do it on the sly, though he couldn't imagine where the fun comes in. " I'll bet you my pater never sprawled like that over my mater," said I, and he said he couldn't fancy his pater and mater doing it either, though he had seen spoony people hugging and kissing like billyo. It's much cooler to-day, but the weather looks less clement. We were kept awake for hours by a thunderstorm in the night. Henry says his sister Polly shows her white feather when there's a storm, but they don't make much odds to him. Haven't had to do any lessons while Henry was here. The mater said I needn't. Grandpa turned up after dinner. Mr. Patmore asked him if he could find that friend of his called Jimmy Cliff, and talk to him, because he was one of those people who thought he wasn't dead. Grandpa said he'd have a try, but it mightn't be easy as the gent may be difficult to meet with. He asked me if I'd seen the old man in the kitchen yet? And I told him I had. He said the old geazer had fallen asleep (died) in his chair, but had got so wedded to the house that nothing would shift him— silly old man, and that people like him were called earth-bound spirits. But at any rate he is a harmless old ghost and doesn't interfere with any one.

Sept. 5.

We went a long walk in the hills yesterday and took sandwiches and cakes and ginger pop for a pic-nic. It was great fun. We saw some great big stones sticking up in one place, and I was able to see (the thought-forms of) a lot of queer looking men dressed in long clothes, sort of praying and doing peculiar things (performing strange rites) which Mr. Patmore said must have been druids. (8). He and Mrs. P. got quite excited at what I told them, and were very surprised at me seeing all that which happened so very long ago. We did a bit about the druids one day in history lesson, but the book didn't say much and I never bothered my head about them. But now I feel different and want to know more. Mr. P. says when he gets home he is going to read about them in the En-something or other and then he'll tell me what he has found out.

115

I got the feeling that the druids were very good men and ever so wise and knew a mighty lot which they didn't tell. (9). After we'd eaten our sandwiches, Mr. P. and I went off by ourselves for a bit to do number 1 and to give Mrs. P. the chance to leave the room if she wanted to, though I recollect Arnold told me once that ladies could go much longer than gents without having to do that. It must be a great convenience. I wish I was similarly constipated (constituted). On the way back we stopped at a farm and managed to get some tea. And my! didn't it taste scrumptious when I was so tired. Mrs. P. does love her tea, and when it gets near the time, intermates that she is dying for it nearly every day. I've noticed that the mater goes on like that too. She says it's the cup that cheers without making people drunk, though she used some long word I can't remember. At all events it's a great blessing when one feels like a limpet.

Sept. 7.

How lovely. The Patmores had a letter from mater this morning. She said if it suited their concerns she would like me to stay an extra week, because she hadn't got a decent servant yet to make do for Janet. I am so glad. Janet got married last month and sent me a bit of her wedding cake, which I didn't put in my diary. I suppose that was grandpa's surprise. (?). (The prospect of prolonging my holiday seems to have produced a masterpiece of careless composition!).

Sept. 10.

A queer looking man with a bald head and a long

116

white beard, dressed all in black, turned up yesterday (in spirit form) and gave us a sermon. He talked very grand, like the Bible, but I didn't think over much of his aura, I must say. First he told me to ask my teacher to pull out his pencil, because he had something important to tell us. So we were all agog waiting to hear what he had to say. He made out that he was a minister, and he looked like one to be sure. This morning Mr. P. gave me for dictation what he wrote down.

Minister.—Hast thou thy pencil in readiness?

Mr. P.—Yes.

Minister.—Then hearken well to my words. Behold it is given but to the elect to hear the voice of the spirits, therefore be thankful to the Lord thy God for the blessings He hath bestowed on thee and the wife of thy bosom through the instrumentality of this boy His servant. Lo, in the days of yore, the voices of the spirits could be heard by the righteous, but in latter days man has turned from the paths of God and delivered himself up to unrighteousness and iniquity, and so hath he become deaf to those who would succour him, having ears that hear not and eyes that see not. Yet God, being a merciful God, hath not left him comfortless, and the time is not far hence when the things that were hidden shall once again be revealed to the humble of spirit who are not blinded by the arrogance of their own ignorance. Out of the mouth of this boy shall issue many truths to be a light that shall shine in darkness and as a beacon to the pilgrim who will but lift his eyes unto the hills. Verily because thou has been humble enough to ask, so even out of the mouths of babes and sucklings hast thou received and shall receive yet more. Nevertheless, unto the boy would I say, beware of pride, and retain thy modesty like a jewel of great price, that it be like unto a crystal reflecting the light of wisdom which we shall give unto thee. Therefore see to it that thou never dost tarnish thy crystal with the vapours of conceit, for the wages of pride are darkness and distortion, but the wages of humility are truth and light. And now, may the peace of God be upon you all. Fare ye well.

When he had gone Mr. Patmore said, " Humff! he sounds rather a pompous old gentleman, and I can't say he's told us anything we didn't know before." So I told him I was of the same mind, and had very nearly giggled when the old gaffer was holding forth. And now grandpa has just been to say it was all *his* doing, and that for fun he'd told the minister to come and give us a bit of a sermon, because he thought it would amuse us. He says there are plenty of *his* sort over there who love to hold forth like that and lay down the law. The minister, he said, had been a preacher (whilst) on earth, and now he didn't want to shut up preaching (even) when he'd got to the spirit world. He told us we mustn't think people changed all of a sudden when they turned their toes up, because they did no such thing. Some spirits took a long time, as we reckon it, to become different (alter their habits of thought). He says a man doesn't change when he leaves off his overcoat, and (similarly) he doesn't change when he leaves off his (mortal) body. Then Mr. Patmore asked grandpa if the minister would be coming again. And grandpa betted he would if we gave him the chance to hold forth. He told us if we didn't want to be bothered with said gent, I was just to take no notice when he comes, and then he won't be able to do anything, and will give over coming as a bad job.

The old minister has been hanging about several times to-day, but I pretended not to see him, and didn't say anything to Mr. Patmore till he had cleared off. Mr. P. says we have had enough of his spiritual platitudes for the present. I don't know what a platitude means, but it sounds all right. To-morrow is our last day here, which is very mortifying as I don't want to leave. But the mater has met with an alteration to Janet, so there is no excuse for me to stay any longer. (I notice by the way, that the more literary I aspired to be at this period, the greater the number of malaprops and distorted idioms.)

Sept. 20.

I am now back in the family's bosom. Ah me, it was hateful leaving Harlech, but there was nothing for it. I still think of that girl with the lovely eyes I used to see on the shore, though I think she left before we did, and now I suppose I shall never see her again in the flesh. But yesterday I made up a little poem on her, and this is what I said:

> Sweet maid I never got to know,
> Wherever thou dost go,
> My heart is with thee.
> Think of me sometimes I prithee
> And then my soul that feels so sad
> Will try to feel a little glad.

I went to the confectioner's this morning for some

Bull's Eyes and saw Janet. She gave me a kiss and hugged me to her chest. She looks very happy and all of a glow and said she had a lovely honeymoon and hoped I liked the bit of wedding cake, and all the rest of it. I don't take to the new parlourmaid as much as Janet, she seems rather sour and hasn't much to say for herself, but perhaps she'll improve with acquaintance. You never can tell, though I must say her aura isn't up to much and looks a murky sort of concern. I have the feeling that fat old Georgina isn't greatly struck with her either. Her name is Henshaw, and that is what we have to call her, though she has got a christian name of course. Pater says she is a very superior person, but I think he will come to rue it. (I seemed to be unaware that the epithet "superior" is not always a compliment). Mildred is quite aimiable. I reckon it's because she hasn't seen me for such a long time. There are to be no lessons till Monday. The mater has a lump (boil) on her nose which is very unsatisfactory. Pater makes jokes about it, but she says it is extremely painful, and I don't wonder. The doctor says it's because she makes bad blood or something. ...Perhaps it's because she doesn't go to the W.C. enough. Papa says when people can't go it's called constipation, and it's an awful nuisance. But one mustn't talk about it in company. As if I didn't know that.

Sept. 23.

To-day I was reading one of pater's books in the library called the Mill on the Floss by George Elliot, and the mater came and took it away from me, though it seemed a very nice book. Mildred says a girl at

120

school told her that George Elliot is really a woman who pretends to be a man, and that some people think her very wicked because she lived in the same house as a man named Lewes, and wasn't married to him. So I said, why shouldn't she if she wanted to? And Mildred said they did things together which were very naughty, but I was too young to be told about it yet. I'm sick of hearing I'm too young for this, that and tother, and wanted to be rude, but pulled myself together. If I don't keep nice to Mildred she'll go and start taking liberties with me again.

Sept. 25.

Mater got annoyed with me at dinner because I passed a remark, and when I reasoned at her she said, Ah well, one day I'd be sorry when she was dead and gone. So that was too much for me, and I said there was no such thing as dead and gone, and that people may die but they didn't go like *she* meant. Of course I was sorry I'd said that afterwards, because she only got in an awful wax and told me I was a wicked ungrateful boy after all the money papa had spent on trying to have me properly brought up and all the rest of it. Then she said if I wasn't very carefull they'd have to send me to boarding school after all, and I'd soon get that nonsense knocked out of me there! So now that is the latest sword of Democracy or whatever his name was, they're going to hang over my head. Well, I'll be jolly careful in future. But I did think it mean of mater to say that about being dead and gone when she knows I hate funerals and every body blubbing all over the place. When I die, I've decided I won't have any funeral. The men who come to clean out the ashpit can cart me away in the night and chuck me into the nearest river, and then there won't be all that fuss . . . . My baby sister still squawks a lot, but at all events she isn't quite so ugly, which is a great advantage.

Sept. 28.

To-day I began music lessons again with Fräulein. She played me a grand piece by Beethoven, and while she was playing it I saw a gentleman in the room who I felt sure was her father. He seemed to have come to listen. He nodded at me and said something, but I could't understand *what*, because he didn't seem to know how to speak English. I wish I could have told her I saw him, but I was frightened to for fear I got into a row again. The mater told Mildred and me when we first started having Fräulein that she had lost her pater and had to give music lessons to feed her old mother. I had the feeling he wanted to tell her he was there, but I daren't, though I do think it's a shame, poor old spirit. I told Fräulein we had been asked to a childrens' party next month, and she said that sometimes she played the piano at childrens' parties to dance to. She said at some houses they wouldn't bother to take up the carpets, which she thought very queer, because she said in Germany people always dance on the bare bottom. Then she wanted to know what I was laughing at, and so I told her that bottom means the thing we sit on, and she had to laugh too, and said she thought it meant the floor. This afternoon I went to see Arnold, but the servant wouldn't let me in because she said he has the mumps, which is very trying.

We are having awful wind, and the trees are fast getting naked again. Oh dear! how troublesome is the thought of another long winter. There has been a lot of bother with the study fire, which *will* smoke and make an awful smell. The pater thinks there may be an old bird's nest up it or something, but mater got vexed and told him that's nonsense, because they had it swept when the place was spring-cleaned. She sent me to the Vicarage this afternoon to ask after the Vicar who has a cold and sneezed in his sermon on Sunday and nearly gave me the giggles. I saw Henry for a minute, who said his pater kicked up a dreadful shindy whenever he got the least bit out of sorts, and always thought he was going to die on the spot. Mr. Patmore says people who talk such a lot about heaven are never in a hurry to get there, and I quite agree with him.

Georgina and Henshaw (the new parlourmaid) have had words and are at daggers drawn, and I hate going into the kitchen now, the (psychic) feel of it is so horrid. They hardly speak to each other except in monoliths. I knew what it 'ud be with an aura like Henshaw's, but if I'd passed any remarks I should only have got remanded (!) (reprimanded). And now the mater is very put out, and says servants are such a trial, and she doesn't know what she'll do, she doesn't really. First of all Georgina said she'd have to go, and then Henshaw went and said *she'd* have to go, and what between the two of them the mater is quite at loggerheads and can't tell whose fault it is at all; though deep down at bottom I'm sure she knows it's Henshaw's. Nurse is on cook's side, and says Henshaw is often that uppish, she nearly drives her distorted. At all events I do hope poor Georgina won't think of leaving us, because she is such a kindly old baggage that if she could help it she wouldn't even say boo to a goose!

Oct. 19.

During biscuits this morning we had occasion to think of grandpa, and lo, he turned up on a sudden and imparted a few things. We had just been having history about the protestants breaking off from the cathlics and the cathlics saying mass for the dead and all that, and we were wondering what grandpa and the spirits thought about it. Then all at once I saw old grandpa, and he said the protestants did quite wrong not to pray for people when they are what we call dead, because unselfish prayers are beautiful thoughts and make a lovely light round the spirits and help them a lot and let them know we are thinking of them too, which gives them pleasure and reminds them they are not forgotten. Grandpa said it is the parsons' fault that so many people (Protestants) don't pray for the spirits, because a lot of them make out that when we die we go to sleep till the day of resurrection, which grandpa says is all stuff and nonsense. He said when he was on earth he felt (in comparison) far more dead than alive, but now that he is supposed to be dead, he feels far more alive than dead. I've just been thinking that if mater knew about our intervues with grandpa and all he tells us, she'd think he was the devil dressed up in grandpa's clothing and come to tempt us. It does seem silly. If only the mater could open herself like Mr. and Mrs. P. to things it would be so much nicer, it would really. I do wish I

124

could see Jesus again. I wanted to ask grandpa all sorts of things about God and Jesus, but he shook his head and said, "not to-day, it was too difficult" (to explain). Henshaw is going soon, and if the mater can't find another servant ere long, Georgina will be left to rain in solitary confinement. I've begun a sore throat and don't feel at all up to the mark. It may come of kissing the cat who has a cold. Pater often remands me for kissing the cat, but I can't help it, she's so soft and warm.

Nov. 8.

Have been ill in bed of a thing called the influenza, which I just had to ask mater how to spell. I am still in bed but able to sit up a bit and write my diary in pencil. The mater is always very nice and passionate (presumably *com*passionate) when I'm laid up. But I have felt awful, and now the pater has got it, because the doctor says it can be very catching. Mr. Patmore has been to see me twice, and even Mrs. P. came once and brought me some jelly. Dear Mr. Wilcox came too to try and cheer me up, and told me funny stories. But Mildred upset me afterwards by telling me that he is leaving our parts in a few months because he has been given a church all of his own somewhere I've forgotten the name of. Ah me! I shall miss him no end. Grandpa turned up several times and seemed to want to comfort me. But best of all I saw Jesus again, who smiled at me so sweetly and made me feel better. The bother is I sort of can't hear properly what the spirits say, when I'm unwell; they seem to be such a long way off and my head feels as if it was full of fog. I'm tired now and can't write any more.

Nov. 12.

I am feeling much better to-day, though I'm not allowed to get up yet. While I've been lieing in bed I've been sort of dreaming about things that seem to have happened ages ago, and as if I was somebody else and yet somehow was me all the time. It's like as if I was remembering things. The people I saw were all dressed up in funny old-fashioned clothes like one sees in picture books and stories about history. I couldn't make it out at all. Then while I was puzzling my head over it yesterday I suddenly saw Jesus and heard him say, though it sounded rather far off, "My son, this is not your first life on earth, for each of us has lived many times before, and what you have seen are memories of the past which have been stored in the soul." He told me I'd soon remember a lot more things, and I wasn't to be upset if some of them are bad. He said people who dön't remember their mistakes make them again, but people who remember them can learn wisdom. And then he told me that what people say is their conscience, is a sort of memory which tries to tell them not to do the wrong things again they did before and got them into trouble, but (that) I shall be more fortunate because I shall (actually) remember the things when I have those kind of (vivid) dreams (or better said, visions) I have begun to have now. After he had told me all this, he gave me his blessing, and was gone. Upon my word, I do love Jesus. But it's a queer thing, I'm not so surprised at what he said about living before, because deep down in my bones I've many a time felt that some of me is very very old. I'm going to be allowed to get up next week.

126

Nov. 13.

Fräulein came to see me to-day, which was very kind. And after we'd had a little chat I said, if only I could hear some music, and she said, "So! Well, you shall if you want to very badly." And then we arrived at the conclusion that if she left my bedroom door open and the nursery door too, I should be able to hear the piano quite well, which turned out to be most satisfactory. But of course the nursery piano is rather a poor concern and doesn't sound as nice as the one in the drawing-room. While Fräulein was playing, I had another of those queer dreams which Jesus says are memories. I was sitting all by myself in a cave nearly naked, and my body was all brown like chocolate, and the weather (climate) was awfully hot. But the lovely thing about it was that I felt so peaceful and happy and seemed to love the whole world. And then I went off into a wonderful dream as if I was in heaven. But I can't tell about it because I don't know how to say it in words. After a bit I sort of came out of my dream, and a darkie with a kind of towel round his head (probably a turban) bowed down before me and handed me something to eat in a bowl. I think I was very aged, and the boy looked after me, though he wasn't my son, but a sort of pupil (disciple). Then some men, also with towels on, came to see me, and bowed before me, and I taught them things which sounded very wise, though I can't remember what I said. But somehow it was all mixed up with what Fräulein was playing in the nursery, and when she stopped it was all over, though I wished it had gone on forever. Afterwards I told Fräulein her music had given me the 7th heaven, at which she seemed very pleased. But I didn't tell her what I had seen, because she might think I was cracked. And now I am going to read for a bit.

Nov. 15.

I have risen from my bed, but don't feel up to much, and always want to sit down. When I walk about I get the pitterpats and can't breathe properly. The pater is still in bed, and mater is feeling poorly, and I shouldn't be surprised if she wasn't sickening for the influenza. Why couldn't we be made without having to have illnesses? I am to start lessons again on Monday, but the doctor says I'm only to have an hour a day for a bit till I'm stronger.

Nov. 22.

I had lessons from ten to eleven only. But I'm glad to say Mr. Patmore stayed on and talked to me afterwards. The mater is in bed with the doctor coming every day. Pater has got up and sits in the study till he feels competant to go to business again. We have a new servant now. Henshaw left while I was ill in bed, and nurse said, good riddance! The new parlourmaid is called Lizzie Bucktrout, but we call her Lizzie, because Bucktrout is such a funny name. I think all names with an uck sound horrid. She is very pretty and I could almost be a bit in love with her if she didn't have to wear a cap and apron and elastic sided boots. But somehow I can't be in love with any body who has to wear those things, they put me off my stroke, as I've heard Arnold say. I wonder if I shall ever play cricket? The doctor says I mustn't run because of my heart, so I don't suppose I shall. There has been an awful fog all day, and what with the darkness and the smell, I think it's intolerant.

Nov. 23.

Last night before I went to sleep, I saw Jesus, and he gave me a great surprise. He said he would come one day soon when Mr. Patmore was here, and tell us something he wanted Mr. P. to write down and give me for dictation afterwards, because there might be things he was going to say which Mr. P. would have to explain. I am so glad about this. I did so want Mr. Patmore to know about Jesus, and of course when I told him to-day he was very surprised and ever so pleased.

Nov. 25.

Wonders never cease! Fancy, I've been wrong about Jesus all this time, and I found it out yesterday. But I don't care. Whoever he is I love him just as much, and if he asked me to crawl on my hands and knees to London town, I'd try and do it to please him, though I know he'll never ask me to do anything so silly. Anyhow this is what I heard him say yesterday, and I repeated to Mr. Patmore, who wrote it down in his short hand and gave it me for dictation lesson to-day.

" My son, it is expedient now that you should be apprised of several things it was neither possible nor wise for you to know before. And first, be not sad if I tell you that I am not Jesus, but another one whose name is of no consequence, but who has been your teacher through many lives.* Although you are a mature soul, remember you have still a young body and a young brain,

* *See Afterword.*

and to have told you before that I am other than you imagined would have served no purpose and merely involved explanations which would have been more confusing than enlightening to your youthful mind. Therefore let it suffice if I say that we who seek to help and instruct those who possess the necessary qualifications, are satisfied to call ourselves the Elder Brothers. Think of me as one of these my sons, or if you so desire you may call me E.B. for short. But judge me by my words and not by what you imagine me to be, for how shall I prove my identity to you who know me not in the flesh? Let it be enough for you to take on faith that I inhabit an Eastern body which I have the power to leave at will and appear in spirit to those who have the capacity to see. That capacity, my son, you acquired in former lives, one of which, an Indian one, you recalled the other day in your vision. For know that the endeavours of one life re-appear as powers or talents in a subsequent one. Aye, verily no effort is lost, and man becomes what he has previously made of himself either for good or ill. Think not as the ignorant do, that man can attain perfection in three score years and ten; in the universe all is a process of becoming; (viz: of evolution) and as with Nature so with man. In your Bible it is written, " as a man sows, so shall he reap "; and therein is contained a profounder truth than men as yet understand. One day ere long, my son, you will comprehend its full significance. Meanwhile I seek the aid of him, who is now your tutor, to explain words I am obliged to use; words with which you are not familiar, and which would take too much time and force for me to explain myself. Moreover I am wishful that *he* should share in the Ancient Wisdom I seek

to impart. For ye two, my sons, have been associated together, and with me, in many lives, though the one has trodden a different path from the other. Do not imagine that anything is the outcome of chance; all is governed by Law, and those ye have loved ye meet again, to rejoice, and those ye have hated ye meet again, to suffer —and if wise, to forgive. Because in the past ye have loved and aided one another, so is it given to you to love and aid one another again; the elder to impart the learning of the world to the younger, the younger to be instrumental in imparting the learning of the spirit to the elder, who is not the less a great and wise soul because in this life he has hitherto been cut off from the light of Knowledge. Bear this in mind, my sons; it is not what ye believe but what ye *are* that weighs with the Exalted Ones, for They look into the heart and not into the head to find the shining jewel. He who hath a great brain may nevertheless have an evil heart, but he who hath a great heart will never have an evil brain, though it may be lacking in forcefulness. Yet when man reaches the goal doth he become great in all things .... And now, sufficient for the day is the good thereof. I give you both my blessing until I come again."
both my blessing until I come again."

When I hear (clairaudiently) the E.B. speak, it sounds all kind and gentle, and not a bit like that old party who grandpa told us was a minister, and who sort of bellowed at us like a bull in a Chinese shop!

Nov. 27.

Grandpa appeared on the scene to-day. We were thinking of him and wondering what he would have to say about living before (reincarnation). And fancy, he said he didn't believe it, and certainly didn't want to believe that he'd ever have to come back to earth again. This gave us a bit of a turn, and we asked him if he'd seen the Elder Brother in spiritland, as Mr. P. calls it. And he said he didn't know about Elder Brothers, but there were spirits called Guides, and perhaps he was one of these. He told us some of them were Red Indians and got into people and spoke through them on earth, and taught them about spiritualism as we called it down here. Well, the next time the E.B. comes we are going to ask him why grandpa doesn't believe about having lots of lives, because Mr. P. says if it's true, it's a queer thing that grandpa shouldn't know about it all. But come to that, even Mr. P. says the idea (of reincarnation) takes a bit of getting used to, and it came as a great surprise to him. Can't say it did to me, though, because I seem to know in me bones that it's true . . . . Mater is still very poorly, and when I went in to see her before lessons this morning, her voice was very soft (weak) and her aura is all grey. I do hope she isn't going to die. She told me to give Mr. Patmore her kind regards, and when I gave them to him, he returned them with thanks, but told me (in effect) that he felt rather awful for encouraging me to do things she didn't approve of at all, specially when she was ill in bed. To-day I feel a bit wormish about it too, and badly wanted the E.B. to come and explain that it's all right, but nothing happened. I'm tired now, and so to bed, like Mr. Pepys.

Nov. 28.

I got a horrid fright to-day. My number 2 was all

132

red like blood, and I thought I must be very ill. But I didn't feel ill; that was the queer part of it. Anyhow, I felt I would have to tell some one about it to ease my mind, so I told Mildred. I wish I hadn't afterwards, because she got anxious and went and blabbed to the mater about it, who sent the doctor to see me at once. He looked at me and felt around, and asked me a lot of questions. Then he said, hum, hah and made a serious face and seemed very puzzled and not knowing what to say. It was all very mortifying. Now I am to do number 2 in the commode, so that he can see what it looks like to-morrow, and if it is still red and all that. And he has subscribed some more beastly medicine for me to take .... I have just seen grandpa. He said, " you look worried, my lad. What is the matter?" So I told him about my number 2. And he said, " I can't see anything wrong with you there. Have you been eating beetroot?" So I said I had, which is quite true. And then he laughed and said something about doctors being nincompoops and always looking for trouble where there is none. " What am I to do about the horrid medicine?" said I. " Throw it down the sink," said he, " and pretend you've taken it." Dear old grandpa, what a relief! to know I am not dangerously ill or something.

Nov. 30.

When I went in to say good morning to the mater to-day, I saw Uncle Willie and another spirit in the room. They were doing something to her to make her better. I wanted to stay and look on, but I'd have only been a nuisance. Besides it was time for lessons, so I had to leave. The mater seems a bit stronger, I'm glad to say.

After milk and biscuits, Mr. Patmore took me for a short walk, as the doctor wants me to get out just a little now I'm more like meself. We met with a child and its mother. The kid had the tantrums, and its mater didn't seem to know which way to turn. So Mr. P. said something about how far more sharper than a servant's tooth it is to have a thankless child. He told me it came out of King Lear. (All the same I hardly think my tutor could have quoted it so incorrectly, even though some Victorian servants were noticeably chary of going to the dentist!). The E.B. came to see us yesterday, and this is what he said: (my tutor having again taken it down and dictated it to me).

"Greetings, my sons! I who receive many of your thoughts know that ye have been exercised in your minds that ye should communicate with me when she who is now on a bed of sickness disapproves of such a course. Yet ask yourselves this, my sons: shall ignorance stand in the way of Knowledge, and prejudice be a hindrance to spiritual advancement? Aye, shall error always be allowed to prevail over Truth, and shall those who can see, obscure their sight because others are blind? Know this, my sons, for your comfort; although in one given life the mind may be unyielding, there is such a thing as making an impression on the soul, which shall bear fruit in a subsequent life. Your mother, my younger son, by reason of her upbringing and orthodox beliefs will belittle and repudiate your knowledge until the day of her passing. Nevertheless the time will surely come, when, however much outwardly she may seek to laugh away that knowledge, inwardly her soul will absorb it for her ultimate enlightenment. Think not, my sons, that I am

134

one of those who deem it right to do evil that good may come. But this do I say; often it is right to do what people *believe* to be evil so that good may come—aye, and to the very ones who erroneously hold that belief. So now ye are answered, and let your minds be at rest .... Is there aught else that troubles your hearts?"

Mr. Patmore asked why grandpa didn't know about living (many times) before. And the E.B. smiled and said:

"Imagine not that those who shed the mortal body become possessed of all knowledge. If ye go to a strange country and dwell in a town, do ye on that account acquire knowledge of and belief in all the religions and philosophies of that country? Nay, instead of embracing them, rather do ye carry your own beliefs and prejudices along with you, retaining them in your mind. And so it is with those who dwell on one of the lower planes of the disembodied. He who was formerly the boy's grandfather inhabits a plane which is a combination of both reality and illusion; and the greater is the illusion because wishful thoughts are immediately transformed into things. On earth, for example, a sculptor may think of a subject, but only when it is executed in stone or metal does it become an object. Not so on what is called the astral plane; for the substance of that plane is so pliable that the subject becomes object almost in the twinkling of an eye. And for this reason, although beliefs may be but errors, they none the less appear to be truths. The peoples of the East, my son, learn the doctrine of reincarnation while still in the flesh and retain its truth when they go to the planes of the disembodied, but the peoples of the West have lost that doctrine because, in days gone by, their priests and prelates deleted it from their creed. And yet one day it will be re-instated, and man shall know the full meaning of "as ye mete so shall it be measured to you again." Let this truth be engraven on your hearts; All is Justice in God's perfect world, and each of us has created his present destiny by his thoughts and desires and actions of the Past — to reap good where he has sown good and to reap evil where he has sown evil. For such is the Law, not of virtue and reward, not of sin and chastisement, but of Cause and Effect . . . . And now I must go hence. Yet one word would I say to the boy ere I go: Love your mother, my son; the more so because it is a sorrow to her that you elude her understanding and are as a lamb which is not of her fold."

(In a much later communication the E.B. told me, in his more melodious language, that if he hadn't come to my rescue when he did, my mother's antagonism towards my psychic findings might have so discouraged me as to hinder my further development. Or worse still, she might have persuaded me that I was the victim of "pathological hallucinations"; and this would have been distinctly bad for my mental health. His wisdom in telling me at so early an age about my mother's limitations and in justifying me in going against her wishes, may seem unusual; but then unusual cases require unusual handling. He also told me that my contact with Mr. Patmore was all in the scheme to counteract the bad effects of my mother's ignorant if pardonable prejudices. Without my tutor I should not at that time have had a single associate who understood my — to most people — bewildering faculties. Besides

which, the fact that Mr. P. could take down the E. B's
more lengthy utterances, was a considerable asset.)

Nov. 30.

An awful thing happened to-day, and I feel all at
sixes and sevens. Georgina had a fit in the kitchen.
Pater said he feared as much, because she has a short
neck or something. Anyhow the poor old body had to
be carted off to the hospital because the doctor said
that was the best thing. Lizzie didn't behave at all
nice, and said she wouldn't sleep in the same room with
a person who was that ill (the servants occupied the
same bedroom) and the mater is far too poorly to do
anything. So nurse had to skewt off and fetch old Mrs.
Prettyman, or we should be left destitute without anyone to cook the grub. I had a feeling when I woke
up this morning that there'd be a visitation but I
didn't know what. Oh dear, I wish I didn't mind things
so much. I don't think Henry or Arnold mind things
half as much as I do. Pater said one day that some
people are born with a silver spoon in their mouths. I
can't say I was. Or perhaps I oughtn't to say that?
No, I know I oughtn't. Think of the poor people who
can't see the lovely fairies and the spirits, aye, and can't
see the E.B. I love so much. And then there is Mr.
Patmore.

Dec. 2.

Appalling news. Georgina has departed this life.
When I heard it I had a good cry. But I know its silly,
because she hasn't really gone, and perhaps I shall be
seeing her one of these days. Even Mildred blubbed a

bit. But of course *she* thinks that when people die they're as good as done for, and its no use *me* saying anything. Even if poor old Georgina turns up I shall have to hold my tongue, though you bet I shall tell Mr. Patmore. (As it so happened I never did contact our old cook after she had passed on. Like my grandmother, she had had very narrow and definite ideas about the after-life, and doubtless gravitated to the heaven of her own making and that of her sectarian associates.)

Dec. 6.

Poor Georgina got buried, and we sent a wreath. I shall pray for her to be happy. Somehow I don't like to go into the kitchen now, it makes me want to blub : and it's awful to hear the parrot do her funny loud breathing when she isn't there any more. I think Tommy (the cat) misses her too, she used to nurse it such a lot. Ah, well?—The Pater says we shall have a job to get a new cook before Christmas, because servants like to stay in their places till they get their Christmas boxes, and then they show their gratitude by giving notice. Fact is, pater doesn't seem to fancy servants very much since Janet left. But he did like Janet though I remember him saying one morn, " When Janet goes, it'll break my heart." Mater is beginning to look more like her old self, but is still confined. The Vicar came to enquire, but didn't come in. I expect he was funky of catching it. A lot of other persons have been to enquire too. This is the result of the mater not going to church. When the pater is ill, people don't come half so much.

138

Dec. 9.

The E.B. paid us a visit, and Mr. Patmore asked him some questions. He said if spirits like grandpa meet Indians who believe in reincarnation—I have learnt that long word now—then why doesn't he believe in it too? And the E.B. smiled, and replied; (in effect) if a Christian meets a Hindoo, on earth, is the Christian (on that account) going to believe what the Hindoo believes? Then Mr. P. said no, he supposed not. But when a spirit comes back to earth, don't the other spirits know about it? And the E.B. said they did not, because the spirits in grandpa's world (i.e. on " grandpa's " plane) went for a time on to a higher world before they came back to this one. That is why a lot of spiritual-ists—what a long word—think people have only got one life down here, and then go on getting higher and higher up yonder, without ever setting foot on earth again. (This of course was only my primitive interpretation of the E.B's words, though I think the sense is more or less correct.) After that Mr. P. wanted to know what made the spirits come back (to earth) again after they'd been up yonder for a while? But the E.B. said he hadn't time to tell us now, and would send one of his English pupils to help us instead . . . So there is a new treat in store for us. I wonder when he will come, and what he'll be like? Mr. P. is to take down what he says, and explain it to me afterwards if I don't understand it all.

Dec. 11.

The mater is up and doing again, but seems to find life an intolerant burden. (A comic malaprop, but, alas, containing a modicum of truth, since "life" is not always graced by the virtue of tolerance!) That new spirit turned up yesterday at milk and biscuits, and afterwards Mr. P. gave me for dic. what he wrote down. Some of it was a bit above my head, but Mr. P. explained it very nicely while he dictated it out to me. I have lessons an hour longer now, because the doctor said I might. We are not going to break up till nearly Christmas. Mr. P. told pater he would make up for the time I was groggy if the pater liked, so the pater thought it very decent of him, and I don't mind a bit . . . When that new spirit was here, the mater swept into the room and upset the apple cart. She came in to say how do to Mr. P. and to thank him for all his kind enquiries and for some flowers his missis had sent. Of course she didn't catch on to what we were up to, which was a blessing, or there'd have been a fine old rumpus. Lucky for us the spirit waited till she cleared out. He is a nice spirit, and looks quite young and jolly and has a very pretty aura. He talks quite different to the E.B. and this is what he said:

"My Master sent me along to try and answer some questions for you. What is it you want to know?"

"Quite simply, I want to know what causes a particular spirit to come back here (reincarnate) at a particular time?" said Mr. P. (My tutor usually noted down our questions as well as the answers.)

"To understand that, you must remember that life is a very complex affair. *You*, my friend, have your physical life, your emotional life, your mental life, and your spiritual life, all of which are intimately associated with and form an integral part of your terrestial exist-

140

ence. You know of course that you have a physical body, because you can see and feel it. But what you don't know is that you have also an *emotional* body, a *mental* body and a *spiritual* body, and that all these increasingly subtle bodies interpenetrate each other *and* your material body. You would realise this if you could see auras. So far, so good. Now to keep your physical body going, you have to nourish and exercise it, or it would be a very weak and puny affair and would soon wither and die. That's obvious. But what about your subtler bodies? Not being composed of gross substance, you can't feed them on beefsteaks and potatoes, so you have to energise and " nourish " them in a different way. If you never felt any emotions, or stifled all your feelings, like some misguided persons do, you'd have a puny little emotional body; and if you didn't develop your mind, you'd have a puny little mental body; and the same with your still higher and subtler spiritual body. Result—after you had shuffled off your physical body on the physical plane, your puny and undeveloped subtler bodies couldn't long survive on *their* respective planes. Now do you see what I'm driving at?"

" Not entirely. What I don't understand is: if my subtler bodies were to perish for want of energy, why would I have to come back to earth, instead of being snuffed out like the flame of a candle?" " Because, my friend, you are an immortal soul, and can never be snuffed out. You think, like the agnostics, who are very fond of using it, that the illustration is apt. You forget that by snuffing out the flame you do not destroy the candle."

' I may be very obtuse, but I still can't see why the

141

soul has to return to earth to become another person?"

"That's because, unorthodox though you are, you have been somewhat influenced by the Church, which has got the whole thing wrong from top to bottom. The Church believes that when a baby is born into the world, God creates a new soul to fit into it's body. I may be maligning the Church, because it's very difficult to know exactly what the Church does believe. In any case, the idea is about as true as to say that a new body has to be created every time to fit a new overcoat instead of vice versa." We both had to laugh at this. "The truth is exactly the opposite. When the soul has shed its subtler bodies, and, so to speak, "died" to the higher planes, *it*, and not some extraneous Power, has to provide itself with yet another physical garment in order to experience the effects of the causes it generated when on earth before. In other words, it has to fulfil it's self-made destiny—for which purpose it incarnates into a given family. Why d'you think that some married couples are childless? Often it's because no soul is desirous of or is permitted to choose such a couple for its parents."

"I see. Very interesting. But do you mean to say we have to go on dying and being reborn at given periods for the rest of all Time?"

"No. Only till you have ceased to generate *causes* on the physical plane which *must* have their *effects* on the physical plane. To give you a trite example. The ordinary man on earth usually saddles himself with business ties, social ties, family ties, and a thousand duties and responsibilities which he can't get out of, and which tie him to a given place. He may take a yearly

142

holiday, but sooner or later he has to return to resume his business activities, pay and collect his debts, and fulfil all his other obligations. Having in the first place created all those responsibilities, he has to go through with them whether he likes it or not. It is the same with the soul, only in a much vaster sense. The soul has created ties and obligations on earth through its desire to make money, have a family, acquire possessions, social standing and many other "treasures on earth". All these are ties which eventually bring it back to the earth-plane, to teach it wisdom through experience. If it has sown evil, it comes back to reap the effects of that evil and adjust its debts through suffering. If it has sown good, it comes back to reap the effects of that good. If it has sown a mixture of both good and evil, as most of us have, it comes back to reap the effects of both good and evil, in which case it's incarnation will be a medley of so-called good luck and bad."

" Then what should the soul do so as not to have to come back at all?"

A very queer thing. After this, the spirit suddenly disappeared and I couldn't tell Mr. Patmore the answer. But perhaps it was all for the best, as the mater loves to say, because I was beginning to feel tired.

Dec. 14.

There has been a terrible stink in my bedroom which turns my stomach. The pater thinks a mouse must have died under the boards, and criticised the cat for not doing it's duty and getting rid of the mice. But I like the poor little mice, though I must say I wish they wouldn't go and die and make such an odious smell.

Anyhow the workmen are here hacking up the boards and the pater complains of the fine bill he'll have to pay. That nice spirit turned up again yesterday, and excused himself for doing a bunk in that astonishing manner. This is what he said and Mr. P. wrote it down.

"You must pardon me for having disappeared so suddenly the other day, but I was called back to my body. As I gave you no reason to think otherwise, I expect you imagine I'm a dismembered spirit? But that's not exactly the case. To be explicit, I happen to be a so-called Anglo-Indian, and I am communicating with you while out of my body which is asleep, thousands of miles away from here. Our night is your day. If it were not, I shouldn't be able to come to you like this. I have learnt to do work on this plane in my *astral* body while my physical body is asleep. Your young companion has the same power, and I often meet him over here. But neither he nor I remember it when we return to our bodies in the morning. Perhaps this seems strange to you, yet it's quite simple. Without special training, the *astral* body does not impress the physical brain with the memory of its experiences. Later on, the boy, who is a more advanced soul than I am, will probably acquire this faculty to some extent. But whether or no, both he and I may be said to lead double lives; there is our life on earth in the day-time, and our life over here at night. Of course if we try to communicate, as I am doing at present, with some one who can *see*—and there are not so many such as yet— there is always the possibility of being suddenly recalled to the physical body by a noise or something which wakes one up; and in that case, one vanishes in the dis-

144

concerting manner I vanished the other night, or rather *day* for you. However—there it is . . . . And now after this lengthy explanation, what is it you were asking me?"

"I wanted to know what the soul has to do so as not to require to come back to earth any more?"

"It has to lay up for itself treasures in heaven instead of treasures on earth. In short, a man has to become selfless, or as the Indian sages have put it, he must become unattached. First of all he must avoid doing evil so as to incur no debts to be paid off in a future incarnation, and secondly, he must do good for its own sake without any desire for reward. Because strong desires, unless unselfish, have sooner or later to be fulfilled, they are fetters which bind one to earth. Strong desires act somewhat like a boomerang; you hurl them forth into time in the shape of desires, and they come back to you in the shape of fulfilments. Say, that in a given incarnation a man strongly wishes for some sort of fame, but circumstances are against him and he dies before his wish has been gratified. What happens? Through his powerful wish, he has generated subtle forces which cannot just disappear into nothingness any more than a boomerang can just disappear into space, so he has eventually to come back to experience the gratification of his wish. And as with one thing so with another. Most people want to be wealthy, to wield power, to occupy high positions, or to shine in society. All these desires, which are actuated by vanity, are the lassoes which catch the soul and drag it back into incarnation. Have I made myself clear?"

"Yes. But am I to understand that all the things

145

you have mentioned are evil, and that nobody ought ever to be rich or famous?"

"They are neither good nor evil in themselves. It is our attachment to them that makes them evil for *us*. Jesus said, for example, the love of money is the root of all evil. My Master says the same thing but uses a different word; he says *attachment* to money is the root of all evil. I know that the Indian idea of non-attachment may seem puzzling to you. Yet after all it is very simple. It practically means that you must not allow yourself to be dependent on external things for your happiness. For the only true and lasting happiness is to be found within, that is to say in the subtler bodies, and above all, in the highest spiritual body which is at one with God. I must go now, or I shall be tiring the boy. Good-bye."

"Well, we certainly live and learn," said Mr. P. when the spirit had gone. But *I* wasn't a bit surprised to hear I go to the spiritland when I'm asleep, because I often have the feeling that I don't just stick in my body doing nothing at all.

Dec. 15.

We all felt horrid at breakfast this morning because pater had just got a letter to say Uncle Robert is very ill. So pater and mater had to pack up and go off post haste to London to see him. He has no missis of his own, and has always been a batchelor like Mr. Wilcox. I suppose he could never meet with a lady he wanted to get engaged to, or perhaps he didn't know how to mash the ladies properly. Anyhow he is very ill now, and Mildred says if he dies he may leave the pater a lot of money in his will, because the pater is his only brother, and he has got no children. I hope poor Uncle Robert won't die, though I have a nasty feeling that he may. Mildred says if he does, we shall all be in the morning and it'll spoil our merry Christmas, which is jolly hard lines. Uncle has got new mownier or new something, and I am sorry to say she says a lot of people don't get better of it. So altogether the whole thing is a bad look out. The mater wasn't at all delighted at having to trip off to London, because she doesn't think she feels well enough to go in the train so far after the influenza. The pater didn't look too grand either. When they left, they said they hoped we'd be good and not get into mischief. I behaved quite decently when I said good-bye this time. I'm better at it than I used to be, and that's a blessing at any rate. I break up with Mr. Patmore on Friday, and am quite sorry.

Dec. 17.

Mildred had a letter from mater to-day with rotten news. When they got to London they found Uncle Robert dead in his bed. If he had lived in our parts instead of so far off, I reckon I'd have been moved to tears. But if the truth be known, we only saw him once in a blue moon, though pater always went to see him when he had to go to London town. Of course I'm mightily sorry for pater at losing his brother, which mater says in her letter is a great loss, and that we were to write at once to our father to tell him how sorry we are, like good children. Mildred says letters of that description are called condolence letters—had to look up spelling in dic.—and that they are beastly hard to write, and she didn't know what on earth she was going to say. Neither did I. So in the end I thought I'd ask dear old Mr. Patmore to ignite (!) me a letter; but he thought that wouldn't do because my parents might smell a rat if I didn't put it in my own way. At all events he did help me with it a bit, and we got it off by the post. Mildred was dying to see what I'd said of course, to be able to poke fun at me I expect. But sucks for her, the letter was in Mr. P's pocket safely on its way to be posted before she got the chance. Not that I'd have shown it to her anyhow. Well, the long and short of it is that mater and pater will be away till over Sunday, and mater wrote to old Mrs. Prettyman to send the pater's black dress trousers off in a parcel at once because the funeral is to-morrow. I suppose mater was wily and took her best black dress with her in case. But perhaps pater didn't want to do that for fear it might look as if he was counting his chickens before they were hatched. Of course now we shall be in for an unmerry Christmas and have to go about with long faces. I do think we are most unfortunate. First, poor dear Georgina goes and dies, and then Uncle Robert on top of her.

Dec. 18.

I didn't feel like writing any more yesterday, so will put in what I missed out to-day. I have broken up with Mr. Patmore, and feel quite lost without him. But he said he would come one day and take me out for a walk, and weather permitting, he will ask me another day to go and have luncheon with his missis. He told me he wanted me to write him a small story for exercise

148

in the holidays, and I said I would. But I don't know what it will be about. I think I'd best write a fairy story about a little girl who went to live with a fairy king or old gnome. No, on second thoughts I'll make her a big girl, because I don't fancy little girls very much, they are so silly and jabber such flapdoodle . . . . It has turned out a disgusting day, all cold and wet and I've been in the pater's study diving into his book shelves. I read some of Mr. Pepys again. He does seem to talk an awful lot about closets. He says in one bit that a " Mrs. Russel did give his wife a very fine St. George in alabaster which will set out his wife's closet mightily." I wonder what he means by set out? The pater talks of setting out for a pic-nic, but it can't mean that. Come to think of it, I don't understand half of what Mr. Pepys is talking about, but I like it, it sounds so funny. Arnold came this afternoon and we played chess. But his pater hasn't taught him as well as Mr. Patmore (taught me). He doesn't keep his eyes open, and I had his Queen when he was looking elsewhere.

Dec. 19.

For once, Mildred wasn't so prone (keen) to attend church to-day, and said if the mater weren't coming home to-morrow and would ask, she'd much rather not go. This made me smell a rat. I believe she can't be mashed any more on Mr. Amery (the curate). Anyhow we did go, and I enjoyed the organ. I wish I had a nice organ. When I'm grown up I shall buy one of my own. Mildred says that's silly, because it would take up the whole drawing room. But what do I care? . . . She is very excited because she'll have to have a new dress now Uncle Robert is dead. I suppose I shall have to have a black coat and knickers too. I wonder if the mater will go into crape? It does seem funny that people should stick on black because some one has gone to have a good time in the spirit land. I call it idiotic, but I daresn't say so to the mater. And all that black makes one feel so dismal, it does to be sure. If I had my own way I'd like to dress in yellow and blue and pink or something nice and bright. I'm sure it would be better for one. Grandpa just turned up here, and said, " You're quite right, my boy." Fancy that now! I asked him about Uncle Robert, and he said, " Don't you worry, we are looking after him. Yes, and he's got someone very special over here who has been waiting for him a long time. Ah, he is very happy to see her again. You mark my words. One day you may hear something and will remember what I've said. But be wise and say nothing now." (Some years afterwards, I heard that my Uncle had had a tragic romance in his life, the object of his affections having died of consumption. Being apparently inconsolable, he remained a bachelor, despite the fact that he amassed a fortune, which doubtless many a woman would have been glad to share).

Dec. 21.

The mater and pater got home yesterday. They both looked a bit long in the face, but strange to say their auras looked a jolly sight brighter than when they went off. (This was not very surprising, considering my father had been left a fortune and my mother had received a very gratifying legacy. As for myself, by the way, I was to be the possessor of a tidy little income when I reached my twenty-first year, and was to inherit the bulk of the fortune after my father's death. But of all this I was not informed at the time). To-day the mater took me out to buy me some ready-made black clothes, and Mildred too. I am now wearing the horrid things. We do look a dismal lot, all in black from top to toe, and the whole place seems to be filled with gloom. The mater is in her usual stew about buying presents for the Vicarage and all that, and complains that it has got so near Christmas and she feels exhausted. Both the m. and p. have to go back to London soon after boxing day to look into Uncle Robert's drawers and give his cast off clothes away to poor people and the like. Mater says it will be very tiring. Pater will have to mess about with lawyers down there, because she says Uncle Robert asked him to be his executioner.

Dec. 23.

Pater brought home a box of expensive cigars for me to send to Mr. Patmore for a Christmas present, and Mrs. P. is to have some flowers. I am so glad, as they are such a deserving couple. Mater has written to Auntie Maud to ask if she can come and stay with us while they (my parents) are away. She doesn't want to leave us alone with the servants for fear we may be up to high jinks. But I have the feeling that Auntie Maud will prove abortive. The pater has been excessively decent and given Mildred and me twenty shillings each to buy Christmas boxes for the servants and each other, and something for Mr. Wilcox who is coming for Christmas grub like he did last year. I was quite dumbfounded, as the pater has never been so liberal before. Perhaps it's because I remember somebody saying that when there's a death in the family it softens people, or something. At all events, it was most satisfactory, and I have been purchasing presents all round, though I had to cuddle my brains to know what to give to each. But that is all finished and done with now, and I hope they'll be pleased with the choices I have made.

Dec. 28.

Christmas is over. I was given some lovely presents . . . (Here follow details which are neither amusing nor interesting enough for publication). I felt a bit sad when the plum pudding came on the table because it was the last thing of Georgina's we shall ever eat. I remember how she invited me to come and stir it for luck that day—and a queer mess it looked. Which reminds me, I have not seen Georgina's spirit yet; she seems to make herself scarce. Perhaps she is going to be like grandma and never come. Mr. Wilcox was ever so nice, but not quite as larky as usual after the pater's sad loss. I couldn't help feeling melancholy when I remembered that perhaps he will never spend Christmas with us again, now that he is to have this new incumbrance . . . Yesterday I spent most of the afternoon reading Dickens. If I ever have to have a nurse, I hope she won't be like Sarah Gamp.

Dec. 29.

I was quite right about Auntie Maud. She can't come to look after us because she has got visitors staying with her for a fortnight or something. So now what do you think? Mater donned her clothes and went off to see Mrs. Patmore, and she and Mr. P. are coming to look after us instead. Crumbs. I am delighted. We shall have some grand times. I only wish Mildred wasn't going to be in the way. We shall have to be mighty careful or she may catch us at it. (i.e. communicating with the spirits). I forgot to put down that on Christmas Eve the E.B. came to give me a special Christmas blessing, but only stayed a few moments.

Dec. 31.

Yesterday the parents went and the Patmores came. They sleep together in the spare room which was got ready all in a hurry. Aperiently they were very pleased to come. (I take it the foregoing malaprop was the result of reading Dickens with a too innocent mind!) A new spirit turned up to-day, and as luck would have it, Mildred was asked out to tea, so Mr. Patmore was able to take down what was said, and I got him to dictate it to me afterwards. Grandpa brought the spirit along, and said, " Here is an Irishman who would like to talk to you. I'll leave him to say what he has to say." Then Grandpa cleared off. The spirit was a rum sort of juggins and talked in a queer way which I couldn't mimic when I repeated it to Mr. and Mrs. P.

" God love you all," he said. " It's a grand thing to be talking to you poor souls who are still caged in your bodies like birds in an aviary who can fly a bit here and a bit there but with no getting away at all at all. And it's a grand thing to be seeing a boy with second sight as keen as the eyes of an eagle, and him being able to see me and hear what's in my mind to say. Ooh, if the

153

blind ones of earth only knew it, it's well-nigh destroyed we are with wanting to tell them we are not just a box of dust in a nasty old grave, but as happy and light as a bit of thistledown floating in the breezes of a summer's morn. Yet there's my old father lamenting and mourning all the light out of his soul, and clasping his hands to heaven and saying, " I've lost my son, and my gray hairs will be going down with sorrow into the grave," and me all the time standing by and telling him " I'm here, I'm here, so let not you be lamenting;" but himself as deaf as a block of stone and blind as an owl in the shining sun. Sure it's a pitiful thing, when the light is glistening all around, for the sons of Almighty God to be groping in darkness and to be fearing death for themselves and their loved ones. But it's the likes of you will be bringing a power of comfort to the world when the days of the great tribulation which the prophets foretell are at hand, and when stricken mothers and wives will get no solace from the prattling parsons. A fine lot they be, may God have mercy on their ignorance, for talking grand things about heaven, and themselves not knowing a shadow of what it is like nor being able to prove it exists at all. And because of their ignorance it's a hard thing they'd be saying if they knew you were communing with the likes of me, and writing down my words of wisdom for their undoing. Ah, they love to be preaching about faith and the love of Almighty God, but I'm thinking it's the seeds of fear they sow in the immortal soul. So let you pray that God and the saints may lighten their darkness and be opening their eyes to the golden rays of truth. It was with gloom and darkness they filled my soul when I was living on earth, and me an ignorant man believing all they said and living in fear of hell. (Presumably this spirit had been an Irish Protestant.)

But let you know that if there be a hell, it's a hell of man's own creating and was never created by God or the Devil. And let you know that this is a world of joy and loveliness, of music and flowers and birds and butterflies, the likes of which you have never known on earth, and the likes of which can never be on earth. Yet this I'll be telling you; beauty on your earth is a shadow of the beauty of our heaven, and it's a bitter thing to have a blindness for beauty on earth, for it makes a longer teaching to see the beauties of heaven. But, God forgive me, I've no call to be telling you this. Haven't I said it's a grand thing to be talking to the likes of you with the shining of truth in your hearts and the milk of human kindness in your breasts?—and you after turning a deaf ear to the parsons and listening to the voices of the spirits instead . . . And now I must be going hence. But maybe I'll come again if you be wanting to see me. May the Lord of everlasting Goodness fill your minds with more wisdom and your bodies with health! God speed you all."

When the spirit had gone, Mr. P. said something funny about him certainly having the gift of the gab, and it was just like an Irishman to do all the talking, but he wished we could have asked him some questions. He wanted to know (from me) what the spirit's aura looked like. And I said it was very nice, and there was a lot of pink and blue, but hardly any yellow to speak of . . . . Mildred came back from her tea looking very red in the face. She has awful chilblains and says

155

they nearly drive her mad with itching, so Mrs. P. condoled with her and said they were horrid things.

Jan. 17.

Mater came home on Saturday, and pater is coming sometime this week. The Patmores left, and I was sorry when they went, because I had such a nice time when they were here. I have started lessons again to-day. Mr. P. was fairly pleased with the story he asked me to write in the holidays, but gave me some tips. He told me that good writers didn't always use the same word for the same thing, but went in for varigations, and that I mustn't always say " he said " and "she said", but sometimes I must put "he replied", " she answered ", and the like. These are called synonyms, he said, and told me how to spell it. Then he gave me a whole crowd of synonyms for "said" because I could only think of *answered, replied, intermated* and a few more. I wrote them all down as he gave them out, so now I know . . . The mater is not all she should be, and looks as if something was upsetting her. But I don't know what, and daresn't ask her. I only (merely) get the feeling that she and pater have started squabbling about some bone of contention. If that's a fact, I wish one's parents wouldn't do it, it's so mortifying, and turns the feel of the whole place upside down.

Jan. 24.

That nice pupil of the E B's turned up this morning for a bit at our 11 o'clock repast, and told us a few things. He asserted that some souls who were far enough on, and didn't want to have to come back to earth again, could become dayvas (devas) or sort of gods or what we imagine are angels. He argued that each country (nation) has it's (national) deva, (I have corrected the spelling here, though the word is pronounced as I originally spelt it) and sort of looked after things, but in a way it would be hard for us to understand. He avowed that Lord Nelson, who won the battle of Trafalgar and said "Kiss me, Hardy," (evidently my own elaborations) was now a (national) deva, and if ever I went to London, I would see him on top of the Nelson monument in Trafalgar Square. (10) (Somewhat badly stated. The Nelson Column is merely his focussing point.) He told us some other things too. He affirmed that some devas who were devas to start with got so attached to a body (viz: a human being) that they didn't want to be a deva any more, and became a person on earth instead, so as to be near the body they loved. He contended that stories about fairies becoming ordinary people like we are and you meet with in fairy tales, are not all flapdoodle (but contain a certain amount of occult lore.) Then he told us the queerest thing of all. He stated that ages ago, I had been a deva, and I (had) so loved the E.B. that he (had) helped me to be (become) a person like any one else who gets born and dies over and over again. But because I'd been a deva, I was able to see things a lot of other people couldn't see, because it was much easier for people who have been devas to see spirits and fairies and the like. After that, he had to go. "Well, well," murmured Mr. Patmore when he'd gone, "it's all very strange. But one lives and learns." "Yes," I rejoined, "now who would have thought of that?"

Jan. 27.

I'm sure there is something in the wind. Ever since the pater got back, the pair of them are always arguing, though not when we are in the room. But whenever I pass by the library door, I hear them going at it like hammer and tongs. But of course I couldn't be such a sneak as to listen. At all events I have got the feeling that there's going to be trouble and a change of some sort and that the mater and pater don't see eye to eye about some'ut. The mater hardly utters at meals, and sort of sulks, and the pater looks vexed at her. Mildred asserts that she thinks the pater wants to go and live in London, and the mater doesn't. But how she knows that, unless she has been sticking her ear to the keyhole, I'm jiggered if I can tell; though I have a feeling she may be right. I remarked to her, "If you think you know so much, then perhaps you'll inform me who is going to win in the end?" "How should I know?" she rejoined, "but you males generally get your own way." "Well, you needn't be insulting," I affirmed. "Oh, shut up," she declared, and went on dipping into her book.

Jan. 29

The new cook arrived. She is no body in particular, but looks rather tight like Miss Griffin used to do, though she bulges more in the upper story. Henry came to tea. He informed me that the Vicar is supposed to be laid up with lumbaygo, but it's really the piles he's got, though I'm not to tell it to anyone. I don't know what the piles are, but Henry says they have something to do with your bottom. I wonder why

clergymen always get things wrong with their bottoms?
I remember Mr. Wilcox had some sort of an affair on
his backside that time he went to bed in our house.
Oh yes, I remember it was called a carbuncle. I'd have
thought parsons would sooner get that thing called
house-maid's knee, because they have to do so much
kneeling down. Have been worriting my head dread-
fully for fear we have to go to London in the end;
because if I have to leave dear Mr. Patmore I don't
know what will become of me. But I'm glad to say
grandpa turned up to-day and assured (reassured) me.
First he asked us how we (had) liked the Irish spirit?
So we retorted that we had liked him very much, and
were amused by his queer way of talking. Then I
asked Grandpa if he thought we were all going to
London? And, God be praised, he rejoined that the
trouble would blow over and ther'd be no London.
(This afterwards proved to be only correct in part.)
Before he went away, he told us that more spirits were
getting to know that I could see them and that my
tutor is interested in spiritualism, so that if some of
them turned up we weren't to be surprised. But they
might not be very good (advanced) spirits, so we
mustn't pay too much attention to what they said. He
contended that a lot of spirits are very vain and . . . .
(I can't read my own writing here, as the script is
smudged and blotted. But probably what my grandfather wished to convey was that many of the unevolved spirits like to " throw their weight about"; which
experience has taught me is true.)

Feb. 2.

While I was at lessons this morning Mr. Wilcox

called to say good-bye to the parents, because he is
going to his new encumbrancy, or whatever it's called,
very soon. But he didn't come into the morning-room
to say good-bye to my face, because he knew I'd be
moved, but said it through the mater instead, for which
I was truly grateful. I do wish he was not leaving our
parts of the world, I shall miss him appallingly; but at
least he has promised to be one of my co-respondents.
The new curate in charge is a Mr. Atkinson, and I
reckon the mater will be chumming up with him before
long and asking him to dinner, but I shall always
remain true to Mr. Wilcox. Lizzie has been given the
sack because mater affirms she is a very wicked girl
and has gone and done something dreadful, but she
won't tell me what. I asked if she had murdered any
body? And mater avowed she hadn't. Then I asked
if she'd stolen anything? And again mater replied no.
Of course Mildred as usual pretends *she* knows, but
won't let on. So as no one will tell me the ins and
outs, there's nothing more to be said. But I'm sorry for
poor Lizzie; she looks so ill, and there's something
queer about her aura. The mater faltered something
about servants being the blain of her life.

Feb. 9.

I have been feeling very tired and achey all over, so
the doctor came along to have a squint at me, and he
says I'm to have a thing called massarje. I am to
lie on the bed, and a lady will come and rub me
from top to bottom, or something of the sort. I hope it
won't hurt. Her name is Miss Ball—a rum name to be
sure. I wonder if she's pretty? Had my music lesson

with Fräulein this afternoon. That spirit turned up again, and said, " I am the father of the lady." But he couldn't say *the* properly, and *father* sounded like what you call people when they make rude noises. He said, " Tell to ze lady zat I am here." So I didn't know what to do, for fear she got angry like the mater. But he kept nodding at me to do it, and I felt sorry for him, because he seemed so anxious I should inform her. At last, I observed when she was putting on her clothes, " Fräulein, have you ever heard of second sight?" " Second sight," she retorted, " no, what is that?" " It's when people can see spirits " I affirmed. " Spirits," she cried, " ach, you are too young to busy yourself with such things, it is unwholesome." " I don't think so," I returned. " I have been able to see spirits ever since I was a very little boy." " Then you have a very large fantasy," was her reply. She does use such funny words sometimes. " Well, may I ask you something?" I exclaimed. " If you wish," she rejoined. " Did your father have a rather fat round face, and hair sticking up on his head like a brush?" I asked. And that seemed to make her jump, and she cried, " yes, he had, but how can you know that?" " Because he is here in the room," I retorted, " and says he is your father." Then she blushed and got quite cross. " It is your fantasy," she affirmed. " If my dear father could come, he would appear to me or to my dear mamma, and not to a stranger. I beg that you do not mention such a thing again. It spoils for me the memory of my father." So after that I felt upset and checkmated, and could only say I was sorry and had meant no harm. (I have since come to the conclusion that many spirits are very poor psychologists. Being free of the limitations of the human body, they forget that the brain is full of prejudices, and the mind full of unreasoning emotions which are extremely difficult to overcome).

Feb. 11.

I had Miss Ball for the first time to-day, and it wasn't half bad. She rubbed me and sort of pinched me all over. She has red hair and freckles and a rather big nose, and isn't much to look at, but she's quite jolly and talks a lot about nothing in particular. I think she gives me something when she rubs me, because I can see it coming out of her. (11) The pater is out of sorts again and complains of the lumbaygo and the horrid east winds. He contends that this climate will be the death of him. Come to that, his aura isn't looking too grand either. We have got a new housemaid called Edith. She came yesterday, and is appallingly plain. I over heard the mater say that she wouldn't have another pretty girl in the house, they only got into trouble or something, or if they didn't, they went and got married like Janet, and then she had all the bother over again. When I told Arnold about it, who came to tea, he affirmed that his pater liked pretty servants, but that Miss Chadwick, their housekeeper, says they are a nuisance because labourers want to come and woo them at the back entrance, or some such words.

Feb. 15.

The Vicar seems to have got over his piles, because he preached to-day. After church, at dinner, I asked the mater what harlots were, and why they were nearer to the kingdom of heaven than pharisees? And the pater pulled a face and said, " Now then, how are you going to answer that?" But the mater was in a fix, and could only look shocked, and told me I was never to use that word (harlot) as it meant something very wicked. This seemed to me a rum thing, because I thought to meself, if Jesus used it, why shouldn't I? After dinner I looked it up in the dic. and all it said was " a prostitute", which left me at sixes and sevens. I must say the dic. can be very vexing sometimes. Mildred didn't know what it meant either, but thought it might have something to do with lying down, because when people lay down they were prostrate. I wonder? I shall ask Mr. Patmore, if I don't forget.

Feb. 24.

We had a visit from a spirit who said her name was Saffow (Sappho) and that she had been a great poetess and wanted Mr. P. to take down some of her poetry and send it to a magazine. I didn't think much of her feel or her aura, and believe she was trying to take advantage. Anyhow this is what Mr. P. took down, because she said it was very important.

> I'm a spirit in the spirit lands,
> All shining soft and bright,
>   Into your world of shadows
>   I send the golden light.
> I send the golden light of truth
> To raise your souls on high,
>   To banish orphans' sorrows,
>   And dry the widow's eye.
> Oh have no fear of dying,

Be you man or maid or boy,
For death is but the passing
To a life of greater joy.

Before the spirit cleared off I caught sight of grandpa, who was laughing to himself as if he thought it a great joke, but he didn't stop to say anything. The spirit told us to be sure and send the poetry to a magazine, and Mr. P. replied that he would see what he could do. But when she had safely gone, he declared it was awful rubbish and that she must have been having us on, or something. He was quite certain she could never have been Sappho, (I have corrected the spelling) who he affirmed lived long before Christ. Then we remembered that grandpa had said some spirits that weren't much good, might be turning up, and that we mustn't pay too much attention to what they said. So I reckon this was one of them. She talked about coming again, and giving us some more poetry. But if she does, we have decided we won't take any notice, like we did with that old josser who said he was a minister. (*Apropos* of " Sappho ", with relatively few exceptions disembodied entities forget their erstwhile earth-names, the memory of which is mostly a matter of the physical brain. Thus any spirit who pretends to be that of some deceased celebrity may at once be put down as a vain or mischievous spook on a low plane.—C.S.) (12)

March 3.

I'm feeling so awful I don't know what to do with myself. Mater sighed at dinner to-day, and said, " Well, your father has decided that he wants to go and live in London, so we shall be leaving here before very long."

164

When she said that I felt as if my inside would all drop out. "And what about me and Mr. Patmore?" I asked. "Mr. Patmore is not the only tutor in the world," she said. "Besides, we might be able to find a suitable school." "I don't want to leave Mr. Patmore," I said. "Its not what little boys want," said she, "but what their parents think is for the best." Why will mater always call me a little boy? I'm not as little as all that. Of course Mildred had nineteen to the dozen to say about it. She doesn't want to leave her school chums, but she thinks it'll be great fun to live in London, where there are all sorts of theatres and concerts and parties and all the rest of it. But it's all very well for her. She hasn't got a tutor like mine who understands when I see things, and doesn't think I'm off my chump like every one else (does). I was so in the dumps all afternoon that I longed for the E.B. to come and say something nice, but nothing happened. Then after tea I saw him all of a sudden, and he said, ' Be not distressed, my son, a way will be found." So after that I felt better.

March 4.

Saw grandpa in bed for a jiffy last night, and he gave me a tip. He said I should ask mater and pater to let me be a boarder with Mr. and Mrs. P., and they over yonder would try to make them let me go to them, like boys go to boarding school. Then in the holidays, I could toddle off to London and be all together. I thought this a grand idea, and this evening when pater came home, I boarded the lions in their den, and begged and prayed them to let me stay behind with the P.'s. Of course I felt all of a tremble while I was doing it, because I didn't know what they'd say, and whether they wouldn't be very angry. But I got through the ideal somehow. Well, the long and short of it is, that at first mater looked sulky and said something about me being fonder of Mr. Patmore than of her. But I said it wasn't that a bit, but I was getting on so nicely with Mr. P. and I mightn't get on half so nicely with any body else. Then pater said, that's all very well, but that the P's mightn't want to have me as a boarder. So did the mater; she said it mightn't be at all convenient. Mater always talks about the convenience. She is always saying to everyone but us, "Are you sure it is quite convenient?" But never mind that. What I was going to say is, that after we had talked to and fro for ever so long, they said between themselves they would think it over. And (meanwhile) I wasn't to mention anything to Mr. P. So that was the end of that. But at all events where there is life there is hope, and to-night I shall pray to God with all my might and mane to soften their hearts . . .

March 9.

I have been living on tent hooks for wondering what is going to happen. The pater is away in Manchester on business, but perhaps something is in the air, because mater was shut up in the library with Mr. P. for quite a long time this morning before lessons. Of course I wanted to know what she said, but he rejoined that the matter was private for the present and that I must wait and see. Why all this dark horsiness? As if I didn't know it was all about me, and whether I'd have

166

to go to horrid London or not. While we were in the midst of lessons, I saw a queer customer hanging about, dressed in a sailor suit, but took no notice because we were busy. But as he waited till the milk came, I told Mr. P. he was there, and we asked him what he wanted, and he said he'd been drowned a short while (ago) and that a cove over there had told him we could help him.

So Mr. P. got out his pencil and paper, and asked in what way? " I want you to give a message to my old ma," he observed. " But I'm afraid we don't know your mother,' returned Mr. P. " That makes no odds,' he replied, " I'll tell you where she's living." Which he did, and Mr. P. wrote it down, though I've forgotten where it was. " Well, I'll see what I can do," remarked Mr. P. " if you'll tell me the message." " Tell her to give over grieving like that," rejoined the sailor spirit. " Tell her it makes me so bloody miserable, and she's no call to go on as if I was a corpse at the bottom of the bloody sea." How shocked the mater would be at these awful swear words. But that is what he said, so I can't help it. Even Mr. Patmore made a bit of a face. Then he (the spirit) said he'd be quite happy over there with his mates if his mother would only stop blubbing, but it made his heart ache to see her in such a state, or some such words. He'd tried to comfort her himself but she couldn't hear him, so had to give it up as a bad job. He finished up with saying, " Tell the old gal to smile. Tell her I'm alive and kicking, and hanging around, if she could only see me." So Mr. P. said he'd do his best, and as she didn't live very far, he'd go this afternoon. Then the spirit gave thanks, and cleared off. When he'd gone, Mr. P. said, " It strikes me I've got my work cut out. I may get more kicks than haypence " . . . It's a pity but what I can't go with him. No, on second thoughts, I'd rather not, it would only upset me. Poor old woman.

March 10.

Mildred and I have been talking. I said, " When pater goes to London what will become of his business?" And she informed me that he would be something called a sleeping partner. It sounds a funny thing to be, and I wonder if she knows what she's jabbering about? It seems Uncle left a large house full of grand furniture, and that's where we are going to live. Mildred is very excited . . . . Mr. P. went to see that old woman, and told me all about it. He maintained that she was the most narrow minded old female he had ever struck and that he might as well have addressed his remarks to a cartload of bricks. First he had to pretend he was a Mr. Jones, and that *he* had seen her son and not *me*, for fear she might gossip and the mater might somehow get to hear of it. I thought this a very wise caution, even though it was a naughty fib. Then when he told her about the message, and that her son had been to her but she couldn't see him, she avowed it was all the Devil's doing, and that her son was dead and wouldn't rise up till the day of resurrection. Mr. P. then monstrated with her, but without any luck; she still saying it was all the Devil. (Finally) after Mr. P. had nearly been talking till doomsday, she went back on herself and affirmed that her son would have come to her and not to *him,* just like Fräulein (had done). So after they'd been a beating about the bush for nearly an hour, Mr. P.

168

had to give it up and go home with his tail between his legs. While he was telling me all this over biscuits, the sailor turned up (himself), and told us he'd been there (at the time) and seen it was no go. " I'll tell you what it is," he said. " It's all those bloody parsons stuffing folks up with a lot of bloody rot as what does all the harm to poor old gals like my ma. Aye, and I'll tell you gents some'ut in return for your kindness, that is if you don't know it already." And he told us there were some parsons over there who were sorry now for all the lies they'd told, and wanted to make amends. Mr. P. thought this very interesting, and thanked him for telling us, at which he seemed very pleased, and took his departure. Crikey! I wonder what the Vicar would have to say to that? And the poor mater too? I believe she'd go up in spontaneous combustion like that old Mr. Thingumybob in Dickens. Had to look up how to spell those two long words in the dic.

March 15.

Hurrah, harray, hurrah! I'm going to be allowed to board with the Patmores. What a stupendous relief. I hardly know how to hold myself in. Of course I shall hate saying good-bye to the mater and pater when the time comes, but I shall be going home every holidays so it won't be so very bad, and not half so awful as if I had to say good-bye to Mr. Patmore for good, like I'd have had to do if I went and got another tutor. Aperiently Mr. P. told the pater that I was getting on so well it would be a pity to make a change and all that. Yesterday he and pater were closeted together in the library for ever so long, and Mr. P. showed the pater some of my exercise books so that he could see for himself. Perhaps grandpa had been at the gathering because this afternoon he turned up for a jiffey looking very cockey, and said, "So you see, my boy, you've got your wish, and we have got ours. It would never have done for you to leave your tutor." Well— all I can say is, I'm mighty thankful the suspense is over, it was making me feel quite sick in the stomache. It was to be sure.

March 16.

I think Mr. P. is as pleased that I'm going to stay with them as I am (myself). What fun we shall have with the spirits and all. "Which reminds me," cried Mr. P., "I'm a bithering idiot! We ought to have asked that sailor a lot of things." Mr. P. declared we ought to have asked him where he was drowned and what it felt like, and all the rest of it. So I said, "Perhaps if we think of him hard enough he'll come back again." But try as we would, we didn't have any luck. I wonder why? .... I am to move into the Patmores a bit before the rest of them move to London. The mater said something about getting me out of the way before they start unmantling the house, or some such word. She seems to be still in the dumps about it all. I expect she's chary of leaving the Vicar behind. But if I were her I shouldn't bother much about pompulent old parson who hasn't a very nice aura and preaches a lot of things that aren't true. But of course she'll miss her friends too, I should be sorry myself if Henry and Arnold weren't still left to me, and so she has my sympathy. It's all very fine for the pater, because he doesn't seem to have any friends to speak of, and keeps himself to himself. If you ask me, he likes his books better than anybody in the world. Of course books *are* lovely, there's no doubt about it, but people are much lovelier, when they're nice. I shall be able to go on with my music lessons with Fräulein now, and that's another blessing I'd have missed by going to London. I love my music lessons, and can play little pieces now by Bach and Schumann. And I love Fräulein too, though she *was* offended with me for telling her that about her dead pater. He still persists in coming to the lessons, and keeps gnawing at me to tell her he's there. But what's the good when she only takes umbrage? I am sorry for him, but I do think he is rather a pig headed old spirit.

April 6.

I got here yesterday in a cab with my trunk. The rest of my things will be put into the furniture van and be transplanted to the new house in London. I felt a bit blubby when it came to taking leave of the old homestead, but I tried to keep up my spunk and not to show it. I didn't have to say good-bye to the mater, as she said she would very likely be coming to see me before they all go off. But I have a feel she may think better of it and stay away. The pater also said he might look me up and have a word with Mr. P. Mildred I said good-bye to there and then. I felt no quarms at leaving the servants, as we hadn't ever become intimate, but I felt it very much at leaving the cat and the parrot . . . . My bedroom (here) is a cosy little room dotted with brickerbacks and there's a little back garden at the back with a tree and some flowers to look out upon. I like the little dining room too. Mr. Patmore has a lot of habberdashery over the chimney piece, which Bridget, the servant, keeps very bright, and (which) makes the room look quite lively.

There are brass jugs, and toasting forks, and bed-pans with long handles, and they are all so shiny one can see one's face in them. I am glad to say there is a nice cat called Fluffy who I took to at once. Bridget is very bucksome and has two cheeks like apples, and dark hair. Mrs. P. says she is Irish. She talks a bit like that spirit who came that day and held forth so much. She seems to be full of fun, and takes liberties with Mr. P. which he doesn't appear to mind at all, and Mrs. P. neither. I know I'm going to be happy here. I like the feeling (of the house), it is so beneficial.

April 15.

Mater and pater didn't come to see me and say good-bye, which was very decent of them, but I got a post card from mater to say they had all arrived safely in London, and were very busy unpacking their things. Mildred wrote me a bit of a letter full of excitement, and said it was a grand big house, and they had a butler, the one who used to belong to Uncle. Yesterday after tea, Grandpa brought along a spirit to see us, who he declared was going to be good enough to tell us a few things, and that Mr. P. should get out his pencil and paper and take down what he said. So Mr. P. did as commanded, and dictated it all to me this morning, so as I could stick it in my diary. Well, this is what he said:—(With the approval of the Diarist's widow I have somewhat doctored, edited and altered the style, though not the sense, of the following two long discourses (see also p. 179) of the Scientist. These did not come through as consecutively in the original as here printed. There were interruptions, irrelevancies and also conjunctions lacking, which spoilt the flow of the language and tended to obscure the meaning.—C.S.).

"On earth I was a man of science. I will refrain from giving you my name, because the sooner it is forgotten the better I shall be pleased. Reason—I made many assertions which I have since come to know were entirely erroneous. I maintained that the disintegration of the body spelt the end of all consciousness," (or as Schopenhauer expressed it: we become but manure for the cultivation of future melons.—C.S.). "A few of my scientific pronouncements were true, it was my negations that were false. I had not learnt to beware of the dangers of inductive logic. Let there be no mistake about it, inductive logic is the snare which has entrapped many an unwary scientist; for the omission of one fact, not to mention a hundred facts, may upset the whole apple-cart of truth. Take the doctrine of Evolution. As a fact it is true, but it has been unjustifiably used as a peg on which to hang many negations, if you will pardon the metaphor. Because men have learnt that the physical organism is the result of a long process of evolution, many have jumped to the unwarranted conclusion that there is no survival after death, and in the attempt to endorse this negation, they say that all ghosts are figments of the imagination, and that because some mediums are frauds all mediumistic phenomena must perforce be fraudulent.

"Then they turn to the New Testament. Finding that

173

the narratives do not all agree, they dispose of all statements relative to survival as due to the growth of legend around the person of Jesus of Nazareth, and say, here is further proof of the extinction of man after death, and of the doctrine of Evolution, as opposed to the immortality of the soul. So you see how great are the dangers of an inductive logic, which conveniently leaves out just those facts which, if they came to light, would render the whole argument null and void.

"And what are those facts? *We*, my good sir, are those facts, *we* are, so to say, the black swans which disprove the erstwhile axiom that all swans are white; *we* are the living refutation of the presumptuous denial of immortality; *we* ourselves survive to refute the negation of survival. But merely because every man, woman and child has not the powers to perceive us, it is argued that we do not exist. This short-sighted argument is based on ignorance of the fundamental principle which governs the Cosmos, and which may be summed up in the one word *vibration*. When the full significance of this is understood—and it may not be for another century—then our existence may be accepted as, at least, a rational possibility. Our spiritual bodies vibrate at a higher rate of vibration than do your physical bodies. And that is the sole reason why you cannot perceive us; and when I say *you*, I mean the ordinary man who has not been born with that special gift which is termed clairvoyance. In other words, clairvoyance is simply the capacity to see those higher or subtle vibrations of Nature which cannot be perceived by the ordinary naked eye. This is what your men of science fail to understand, and instead of investigating the nature of clairvoyance, they dismiss it, and repudiate it as unworthy of their great intellects!

" Ah, those colleagues of mine! How painstaking and scientific they are when dealing with their own subject and how unscientific and careless they become when dealing with phenomena outside their special domain of research! Specialism, my dear sir, is not the friend of truth, but its foe. The facts which a specialist collects may be true, but the conclusion he draws from those facts is generally false . . . . Permit me now to say a few words about Space. You look up into the firmament and you think it consists of empty space dotted with stars. That is an illusion due to the limitations of your five senses. There is no such thing as *empty* space; it only *appears* to be empty because of the rarity of its matter and the rapidity of its vibrations. For instance, to *you,* my good sir, the space which I occupy in this room would seem to be empty, but not so to your young companion, for he has the power to see me occupying that space. Although the matter of which I am composed is too subtle for *you* to perceive, it is not too subtle for *him* to perceive with his extended range of vision. Thus you see that Space, which appears to be empty, may not be empty. Therefore if I tell you that, just as in the province of machinery, there are wheels within wheels, so in the Cosmos there are worlds within worlds, my statement should not seem to you as utterly unreasonable or impossible to accept. Nor should it seem unreasonable if I say that I can occupy the same space as some material object or physical body. Here is a chair. I now move forward a little and I interpenetrate this chair, for the atoms of which the

175

chair is composed are sufficiently far apart to permit of my so doing. It is something similar to your capacity to walk through a fog. You on your earth only know of three dimensions of space, but we in our world know of further dimensions, for which there are no words in your language. You have length, breadth and height, but we have yet another dimension which might be termed throughth . . . . Is there anything you wish to ask me?"

"Yes, I would like to know," said Mr. Patmore, "what it is that is speaking to us? Is it your soul?"

"No, it is one of the, shall I say, garments, of my soul. Later on I shall shed that garment, and live and move and have my being in a yet higher world of consciousness the vibrations of which are still more rapid and the substance of which is still more rarefied. And here is a point that is worthy of note. All progress is a step towards greater happiness. You in your world do not know what happiness is, you merely get the *reflection* of true happiness . . . . Now I must bid you good-bye. I trust that I have been of some service to you?"

After that he disappeared. When he had gone, Mr. P. said it had been most interesting, and he was sorry Mrs. P. hadn't been there, but she was at a mothers' meeting or some such silly rot.

April 23.

The piano here is a pretty awful concern. Mrs. P. says it belonged to her grandmother, but Mr. P. says it must have come out of the ark. When I'm practising all by myself, Bridget sometimes comes into the room

176

and says: " Now wouldn't you be playing something lively with a bit of tune in it?" Poor Bridget doesn't fancy classical music. When I ask her if she can play the piano, she says, " I can not, but I can play the concertina and the mouth organ." But when I requested her to produce out her mouth organ and tootle me something on it, she cried, " Sure I would not play to the likes of you, when you can make such grand noises on the piano the way would rejoice the ears of God and all the angels." She's a rum customer is Bridget. Mr. P. says it's called blarney . . . I have to go to Fräulein's place for my music lessons now, as Mr. P. has boys here on Tuesdays and Fridays in the afternoon and it worrits them. Fräulein lives in a very small house with her old mother, who is deaf as a pike, and suffers from the blithers, and can't keep still a second. I think she has got the dropsy or the palsey or whatever it's called but I wouldn't be sure. The old father hangs about the house all the time, and keeps making signs to me. I wish to goodness I could tell him there are nicer things to do in spiritland than glueing himself to Fräulein's apron strings all the livelong day. I think I shall ask grandpa to try and do some rescueing work.

April 27.

This afternoon when Mr. P. was out doing his teaching, I sat in the wee garden with my pencil and drawing book and drew a lot of pixies and gnomes by heart, like I often do. Then out came Bridget and said, " Let you be a nice boy and show me what it is you've been drawing there." So I did for fun, and she went into such ruptures and let out such a fountain of

177

words that I wondered wherever she could produce them all from, I did really. I wish I could find such a lot to say about something. When I've said it's nice, or lovely, I seem to get stuck, and can't think of anything more. But Bridget can go on for half an hour, till it's almost like being on a merry-go-round. When Mr. P. got back from his teaching, I thought I'd show them (the drawings) to him as well, and he said something about me having real talent, and that I ought to have proper lessons if the pater would consent. Well, the long and the short of it is that he thinks he'll write to the pater and ask if I can have a Miss Wilson who lives in the proximity, and then we'll have to see what he says. It ought to be great fun if she's a nice party . . . . That silly spirit who calls herself Sappho turned up again. But once bitten twice shy, so we gave her the cold shoulder and pretended not to notice. I didn't think her bit of poetry was so awfully awful, but of course Mr. P. knows better, or I suppose he does. Mrs. P. is not quite up to the mark, and has some itchy spots which she contributes to the Spring.

May 3.

The pater wrote and said I could have Miss Wilson, so that is most satisfactory. Mater enclosed a letter, and declared they were getting more settled, and hoped I read my Bible and was attentive at church. I think the poor mater has got church on the brain. Well, I don't much fancy the church Mrs. P. takes me to; the music was nicer at the Vicar's. I asked Mr. P. why the clergyman always says Gad instead of God, and makes knowledge sound like no ledge, and Mr. P. rejoined that it's because the man's an affected ass. I wonder why Mrs. P. sits under him? . . . . There is a chit of a lady called Miss Swan who's always coming to the house. Mr. P. says she worries his life out with wanting to read him things she has made up. To-day I saw her in the passage, and she's got a being sort of stuck in her aura (i.e. she was obsessed by a deva) rather like that Miss Salt at Birkdale, only it's not an old gent but a kind of big fairy. Mr. P. declares she wants to change (reform) the world, and writes things in old-fashioned words something like the Bible with water. But she's an awful egoist really; though I had to ask him what an egoist might be when it's at home, and he told me it's some one who is taken up with their own importance, and thinks no end of themselves when they've no call to do it. When I mentioned about the fairy, he got quite excited and wanted to know a lot more. But I couldn't tell him, because I'd never seen a fairy sticking to a person before like that. (13).

May 11.

First I had Miss Ball and then I had Miss Wilson, so I've been busy this afternoon, and no mistake. I always feel better when Miss Ball comes now, though it used to tire me before, even though she gave me something (force) and I felt better afterwards. Miss W. is a bit like a sparrow. Her nose sticks out like a beak and she has little black eyes something like the buttons on mater's kid boots which I used to have to button up for her when she couldn't be bothered to stoop. Mr. P. says boot-button eyes are well known. I never knew that before. Miss W. brought a book with draw-

179

ings of this, that and tother which I have to copy. I'm to begin on some flowers, but I'd much rather draw things out of my head. Yesterday evening, that spirit who said he used to do science, came and gave us a talking to. I thought it a wee bit dull meself and didn't want to stick it in my diary, but Mr. P. said it was very interesting, and one day I should think so too, and I ought surely to put all the things down and keep them carefully, or else later on I'd be sorry I hadn't. So here goes.

" As you have done me the honour of thinking over what I said the last time I spoke to you, I have come again. It is a great satisfaction to me to find this medium of communication which enables me to contradict some of the fallacious statements I made while on earth. I mentioned Evolution when I was here before; but although your men of science are putting forward a truth as far as it goes, it is only a half-truth as they understand it and expound it. They are pre-occupied with the evolution of Form, and overlook the much more important evolution of Life. They maintain that the form is actually responsible for life or consciousness, simply because the more complex the organism the higher the state of consciousness. Thus they say that a man has more consciousness and more intelligence than a frog, because he has a more complex and refined organism; the form being the cause, the consciousness the effect. The deductions they draw, however, are erroneous. Life can exist entirely independent of form, and the latter is merely responsible for the particular manifestation of life within a given form; in other words the question is not one of kind but of

180

degree. For instance, if the sun's light shines through a piece of smoked glass, its vibrations are impeded, and it appears to be dim. But if it shines through a piece of clear glass, it appears in all its brightness. Yet it is the same sun through whatever sort of glass it shines, and the glass itself or colour of the glass does not create the sunlight in the first place, for the sun exists apart from any media its rays may happen to penetrate. As with light so with life. Life is eternal and omnipresent, forms are merely concerned with its particular and peculiar degree of manifestation. This is what your men of science will one day come to realise. Meanwhile they are the victims of yet another fallacy consequent on the drawing of false deductions. They believe and assert that life can exist apart from consciousness. They say a tree, for example, has life, but it has no consciousness. We over here know that to be false: we know that even a tree has a dim consciousness as long as it is alive, and hence is a suitable medium for the manifestation or ensoulment of a certain degree of the omnipresent Life.

" And there is another point. Your scientists only know of one scheme of Evolution, but there are two. There is not only the evolutionary scheme of physical Nature, there is also the evolutionary scheme of the nature spirits, which, knowing no better, the men of science dismiss as superstition. Ask one of these hard-headed gentlemen to believe in what are popularly called fairies, and he will say that you are insulting his intelligence. But had he our vision, he would know that what he considers his immunity from superstition is merely ignorance due to the limitation of his five senses. Yes, my dear sir, he would be very surprised to learn that each element has its denizens, and that there are fire-spirits, and water-spirits, and air-spirits and so on, and that the two latter species have a certain amount to do with weather conditions.

" Nor is this all. He would be still more surprised to learn that the sun is the physical body of a Great Spirit, and that the ancient sun-worshippers were not just a lot of superstitious ignoramuses who were worshipping a myth. Moreover, the planets, including our earth, ensoul the spiritual bodies of great Entities known as the Planetary Spirits—a matter which if appreciated would throw a very different light on the ancient and recondite science of Astrology; a science which your savants repudiate as an exploded superstition worthy to be classed with the belief in evil spirits and such like supposed-to-be-figments of the imagination. They argue, with seeming justification, that it is impossible for heavenly bodies, calculated to be billions of miles away, to affect the destinies of man —all of which may sound very rational, but merely so because certain revealing facts are left out of the argument. What the savants fail to understand, is that it is not the stars themselves which affect human destiny, but the magnetic forces emanating from the Planetary Spirits which ensoul those heavenly bodies.

" Yet mark you this; the day is not very far hence when Astrology and other of the recondite sciences will come back into their own. Modern enlightenment is little else than a mask for modern ignorance! But even ignorance is finally dispelled by knowledge, and so it will be in the end. Nevertheless, this type of ignorance masquerading as enlightenment is one of the concomitants of the conquest of Matter, about which I have received a certain amount of information since leaving the earth. Reflect for a moment on the trends of the great civilizations of the past. The great civilization of ancient India aimed at the conquest of Spirit, and its Sages bequeathed to posterity systems of metaphysics which have never been surpassed, and before long, by the way, will come into prominence in the West. Then there was the great Egyptian civilization, which, before it began to decline, aimed at the conquest and understanding of what is called the *astral* realm; a realm which has nothing to do with stars as its name suggests, but is one of the lower planes of the disembodied. In the Egyptian Mysteries, the neophyte was taught how to leave the physical body and contact the astral regions while the body was entranced. Thus, whereas the Indians specialised in Metaphysics and Mysticism, the Egyptians specialised in what is termed Occultism.

" Then finally we come to the great Grecian civilization. Both India and Egypt had been chiefly concerned with the superphysical, but Greece was concerned with the physical and what we may call the conquest of Matter, or rather, I should say, with the beginning of the conquest of Matter. This took the form of love and portrayal of physical beauty. Yet as the centuries went by and Greece declined, the conquest of matter assumed an entirely different aspect, and the age of machinery dawned. Even now it is only the beginning of the machine age, and one of you will live to see inventions that would have staggered the minds of your forefathers. We in our world know certain things in advance, for the programme of progress, if indeed progress it can be called, is to some extent before our eyes. Remember that ideas do not originate in the material world, but in the world of ideas which we inhabit.

"An idea exists in *our* world before it materialises in *your* world; and that is why we are able to foresee the trend of thought and activities on your earth with a certain measure of accuracy. We often make mistakes as regards time, I admit, but then it is difficult for us to estimate time as you understand it. Moreover, the scheme of things sometimes has to be changed in parts owing to the moral backwardness of men and the vagaries of human nature. Bear this in mind and do not criticise us too harshly when our predictions are not fulfilled . . .

"And now I have given you enough to digest for the present, and will bid you good day. Thank you for your interest and patience." I suppose this is all very clever and that, but between me and the gatepost, I do wish he'd draw it mild a bit, it does make an awful long dictation for a chap. And besides, I got tired before he'd finished holding forth. I like the other spirits better; they are much more fun. But never mind, Mr. P. thinks it's ever so interesting, so what more do I want?

June 2.

Dr. Bolton came and had a squint at me to-day. He pretended he was passing and just popped in to say how do, but as he pulled out his concern and sounded my chest, (I don't know what it's called) I expect the mater sent him on the sly . . . . I got an abusive letter from Mildred this morning, full of explosives and injections. She complains that I haven't written to her for ages, and says I'm a skunk. So I sat me down and put pen to paper and hurled some mud at her in return for her kind attentions. I've shown her that two can play at that pastime. There's a Miss Midge who comes here and pays visits. She does talk silly and go on in a soft way. I wonder why hens always cluck after they've laid an egg, and some women always snigger after they have past a remark? Mrs. P. calls it nervousness, but I happened to overhear Mr. P. say that the woman wants ravaging. I don't know what that means and don't like to ask, seeing as I wasn't supposed to hear it.

Aug. 2.

I have been here nearly a week now, but had no time to write in my diary. London is a huge place, and I feel quite as sixes and sevens. We have a grand house in a part called Belgravia, and live in a terrace, with a butler to match. My bedroom is nearly at the top, and I get quite out of breath climbing all those stairs. But it is a nice room, and I've got a table where I can do my writing. Somehow I don't like the feel of where we live, though I don't know how to say what is the matter with it. The feel of the house isn't very nice either, but I don't tell the pater and mater. I think the pater is very pleased with himself about it, and enjoys having the butler and the servants. There are four of them altogether, but I haven't got intimate with them like I did at home when Janet and

Cookie were there. Mater doesn't want me to go messing about in the kitchen now and chumming up with the domestics as pater calls them, but I have had one or two chats with the butler in his butler's pantry. He is quite a decent old sort, though a bit full of airs and graces at times. He gives me now and then some fruit on the sly, which I find very delicious. Our meals are much grander now, and there is always some desert on the sideboard, but nobody seems to want to eat it except me, and I'm not allowed to, save on Sundays, so I suppose it's only for show; perhaps because Cousin Agnes and her mister are here, Cousin Jimmy. It is nice having them, as they take Mildred and me about to see the sights. We have a carriage and pair now, and go driving in Hyde Park. But when the mater wants to use it, we have to go in the omnibuses which I like better because we can ride on the top. We went to the Tower of London yesterday, but the feel of the place was so full of horrors it nearly made me reach and part with my luncheon.

Aug. 7.

To-day we went to the National Gallery to see the pictures, and I was carried away. I have quite decided that I want to be a painter when I'm grown up. I wanted to sit down in front of the pictures I liked most and just *feel*, but the others wanted to be always on the go, and so I never got a chance. I reckon if I'd been left to meself, I would have had one of my big dreams, (visions) and I felt very annoyed I couldn't. We saw the Nelson monument in the middle of Trafalgar Square. That spirit was quite right, there is a big being (deva) up there, with lovely colours. I did so want to stop and look at him properly, but if I'd asked to, Cousin Agnes and Cousin Jimmy, let alone Mildred, would only have thought me dotty. What a disadvantage relations can be. It really makes everthing all very difficult. The heat this afternoon was something stifflicating and the only bright spot was when we went and had ices. I am longing to ride in the handsome cab, but they only hold two, and we are four. How London does smell of horse dirt, it almost smothers one at times. There are boys who run in among the horses and carriages and brush it into a dustpan or whatever it's called, and I get frightened lest they may be run over. My baby sister has got to the dumpling stage, and looks " ruddier than the cherry." The only thing I don't much like about being born so many times (reincarnation) is that I shall have to go through *that* again. It irks me enough to be a young boy, but to think I shall be a little baby who can only dribble and scribble and piddle is a most mortifying idea. Cousin Agnes and her bridegroom still seem very mashed on each other even though they *are* married. But I have a feeling that they're divinities. (Surely I meant affinities?)

Aug. 14.

Cousin Agnes and her helpmate wanted to go to church in St. Paul's cathedral yesterday, and took Mildred and me. I should have quite liked it in that grand place, only the music was such a jumble. Cousin Jimmy said it was the echo that spoilt everything. Most unfortunate. The mater has chummed up with a lot

187

of new parsons *as usual*, and some of them invaded the premises for supper last night. The mater and pater are finding their grand house such a new toy that they have decided not to go away for a holiday but have people instead. The Vicar and his missis are going to stay a few days on their passage through to Eastbourne where they'll be holiday making. But we shan't see them, because Mildred and I have been asked to go and look up Aunt Caroline and Uncle Alfred for a fortnight at Brighton. It's so long since I've seen them that I'm wondering what they've grown into. Well, whether or no I shall enjoy being by the sea, and they tell me Brighton is a very lively place with Punch and Judy shows and all. We went for a walk in Rotten Row this morning and saw all the grand people dressed up to the nines. I have to wear my Eaton suit in London to match the others, but find it almost intolerant when the weather's as hot as it has been. As a matter of fact, James (the butler) told me that all the swells were out of town, because the season ends in July. I believe he thinks the mater and pater are not behaving properly because they have stayed behind, though he didn't put it into so many words. The pater is getting a protuberance, even though he declares that he takes plenty of exercise and walks in the parks every day. The mater seems to have got a bit enlarged too. I expect she sits too much in the carriage and pair. You never can tell. I had a jolly letter from Mr. Patmore. He says they are at Cromer smelling the poppies which make them feel quite sleepy. Mrs. P. has latterly been suffering from that disease when you can't go to sleep. It must be very tiring.

The loving couple, as the pater calls them, have departed hence, and I managed not to blub when I said good-bye. I went for a little walk by meself, though I'm not allowed to go far, and felt things. (psychically sensed up things.) I like looking at persons' auras to see what I can see. Some quite common people have nice auras and some people who are dressed up to the nines have horrid ones. Most men have a lot of dirty red round their middles, and some women too. But I don't know what it means. To-day, as I passed two ladies in the square, I heard one of them say, "I suppose you noticed that Clara is in an interesting condition." So at luncheon I asked the mater what it means? And she looked a bit funny, and went red and didn't seem to know what to say, so told me not to ask so many questions, which was hardly fair because it was the first question I'd asked. James sort of bit his lip, and then suddenly left the room. I don't mean he went to the closet, I only mean he cleared out quick march. I do think it's a bother you can't say leave the room without meaning you want to do something. But never mind all that. When he had gone, the mater said quite cross, "I do wish you wouldn't ask questions when James is in the room." "Well, he's not in the room now," I contended, "so I think you might answer me." "You'll understand when you're grown up," she replied, and omitted to tell me any more. The same old excuse! But I can guess what it means. The mater dresses much grander since we've come to live in London. What rum things fashions are. Why do ladies have to wear a funny thing called a bustle which accents their backsides? Mater says that, Vicar permitting, I can have Henry to stay with me for a week or so when we get back from Uncle Alfred's That'll be great fun, and we'll go and see all the sights together. Grandpa turned up for a moment last night when I was in my bath, and asked how I liked the new house? So I replied it was big and grand all right, but it had a dismal feel as if somebody in the dumps had lived in it. Then he rejoined that Uncle had been a lonely and unhappy man, and that's why. But I answered, " I don't see how he could have been all that lonesome, because crowds of his friends have called on the mater, or so she says." To which he remarked, " Acquaintances, my lad, not friends. A man may have many acquaintances but no one he can call his friend. He only loved one soul in his life on earth, and she died. It is never wise to put all one's eggs in one basket " Then he said he'd come and tell us some more about love when I got back to my tutor's. I asked him if Uncle was happy now, and he said he was, because he is now with the soul he loved. " He hasn't favoured *me* with a visit," I observed. " No," said grandpa, "he wants to forget all about his life on earth." " If he hadn't any friend," I declared, " I wonder why he wanted to make so much money, with nobody to spend it on?" But Grandpa told me he did it, sort of to try and forget his dumps, and because some people like making money just for the fun of (making) it.

Aug. 24.

We got here on Friday. The mater saw us off at Victoria station, and told us we must amuse ourselves

190

and give Aunt Caroline as little trouble as we can. She gave me five bob to spend on going on the pier, and seeing the performing fleas, and subscribing to the niggers and Punch and Judy shows and all the rest of it, and she did the same to Mildred. But she said we weren't to go and buy a lot of sweets with it. When we got to the end of our journey, which I enjoyed except for the long tunnels which produced an awful noise and stink, Aunt Caroline was waiting on the platform with a cab to take us to our destination. (Even in Victorian days cabs didn't usually come on to the platform, but that is a detail.) I like Auntie C. and Uncle Alfred, and they both made us very welcome. Their house is on the promenade, and my little bedroom looks out on to the sea, which is a great convenience as I can see the people walking to and fro and watch the ships and all. As soon as we got into the house, Auntie asked if I wanted to make myself comfortable, and I shouldn't have known what she meant if she hadn't said it in a sort of whispering (confidential) way. Auntie isn't quite fat, but she has plenty of covering, especially at the front. Uncle Alfred has grown into a large man since I last saw him, and has rather a blotchy red face, but he seems very good natured and makes a lot of noise when he laughs or blows his nose. He smokes great big cigars which smell very nice when he starts them and stink something awful when he has finished them. He seems to spend most of his time playing at golf somewhere. Auntie told us we could amuse ourselves in our own way as long as we were in in time for meals. So Mildred and I usually part company. She likes to go into the town looking at the dress shops, and I like to watch the niggers and Punch and Judy and the ventriloquist from the promenade, though best of all I like to listen to the band or watch the waves rolling in when the tide is well up. How lovely the air does smell after all the horse dirt in London. Yes, I like Brighton. It's a lively sumptuous place with it's long promenade and big hotels, though I wish they looked old like Harlech castle or those old places in York. I shan't write much in my diary unless it's wet, because I can't spare the time.

Sept. 16.

I haven't been writing much in my diary for varied reasons. When Henry was with me in London we were on the go all the blessed time, though it was exceedingly pleasant. We went to the Crystal Palace, to the Wax Works, to Kew Gardens, the Zoo, and ever so many places, and Henry enjoyed himself hugely. Because he's the Vicar's son, mater made no end of a fuss of him and wanted him to see as much as he could. So every morning we had a different projection (project) and mater gave me money to pay for everything we did, and declared, "Now whatever you do, don't let him pay for himself." Not that poor Henry *could* have paid for himself in any case, because if the truth be known, his pater doesn't give him much by way of pocket money, as the Vicar isn't supposed to be very well off himself. In the new house Polly cohabits the day nursery, and sometimes when Gladys has gone to bed, Henry tried to teach it to belch. It has learnt to make baby noises like Gladys, but it still mimics the late poor Georgina who I've never seen once since she kicked the bucket into spiritland.

Henry and I travelled back together, which was great fun, and made it easier for me to say good-bye to the mater. Mr. and Mrs. Patmore met me at the station here and gave me a grand reception. It was simply ripping to see them again, and their little house feels ever so much nicer than our huge concern in Belgravia which is so full of the dumps. When we got home, Bridget gave me a great sounding kiss and let out one of her fountain of words on me which I thought would never stop, though it warmed the cockles of my heart, it did. She had cooked me a special cake in my honour, which was very moving. The P's both look well and brown, and Mrs. P. has got rid of not being able to fall asleep. We started lessons again today. I am finding shorthand a fair coughdrop to swallow. Next week I shall be having Miss Ball, Miss Wilson and Fräulein, so my work will be cut out. But I shan't mind that.

Sept. 19.

Yesterday Grandpa came and gave us that talking to about love. He says in the spirit world it's love what counts, and the grand people there are not the folk what used to be dukes and duchesses and Sirs and Ladies, but the people who shine the most with the light of love. He said we ought to try and feel loving to every one, be they ever so humble or ever so wicked, then we shall be all the happier on earth and ever so happy when we get to the spiritland. He said lots of people (on earth) are sort of ashamed to show their love and try to smother (suppress) it as if it was something wrong or milk sloppy, and they oughtn't to do that, because love is the most beautiful thing in the world. He says it is love that holds the world together, and if God was not Love, the world would all go to smithereens. He told us that when we meet some bodies we don't like, we should say inside ourselves, peace be with you, many times, and after that we'll feel quite different about them. He said he was sorry he hadn't loved more bodies when he was in our world, but he'd had it knocked into his head that you can't have many friends, and can never be fond of a lot of people, but only a very few. Grandpa says now that that's all fiddledeedee and that when people can't be fond of a lot of folk it's simply because they haven't much love in their hearts, and can't see the good in others. He says it's often just a silly pride that makes people like that, and they ought to learn to be more humble and feel kindly towards every one. Good old grandpa! . . . . Fluffy has had kittens in the scullery cupboard, and Bridget had to drown three of them in a bucket, which she didn't like at all. I'm glad that *I* hadn't to do it. We are keeping one, and they are going to try and find a home for the other. Bridget has talked twenty to the dozen about those kittens. She held forth till Mr. P. had to shoo her out of the room.

Date Missing.

I've been trying to paint lovely views out of my head with mountains and fairies and all, but when I wet the paper it all went into lumps and got out of hand, and I lost my temper, and said, drat the blithering thing, and tore it up and drew instead. I asked Miss Wilson to-day when I could begin to paint, and she said first I must learn to draw correctly. Had my music lesson with Fräulein. Her pater is still hanging about the place. She and her mater have been to Germany for their holidays, and hoped one day I would go to Germany too, because she says it is so much more beautiful that England, with no fogs and such a lot of wet. Bridget is a Roman Catholic and goes to mass on Sundays, and so I asked Mrs. P. if I could go with her just to see what it was like. And Mrs. P. said she thought the mater would be shocked, but I could go just this once, so off I went yesterday with the volatile Bridget. Well, I was mighty surprised at what I saw, though I didn't understand hardly a word of what the man was saying, because it was nearly all in Latin except for the sermon. Things happen much more than in our church, where nothing much happens at all. At one bit of the service a sort of huge church got built up, (I saw this clairvoyantly) and then a lovely shining Being came down and filled the whole place like an angel, and I felt all peaceful and lovely like as if I was in heaven. I wish I could always go to mass instead of to our church, but of course I can't, or there'd be a row. And fancy, I've found out that Bridget believes in fairies, and says in Ireland there are little people called leprecauns what are up to all sorts of mischief if one gets on the wrong side of them.

Sept. 24.

I've been a bit in the dumps to-day. I've got the feel that I'll never be able to do things like other boys, play games, climb mountains and go for great long walks, because of my heart. And even when I'm grown up I shan't be strong. I call it beastly hard lines, but I

suppose I shall just have to stomach it as best I can . . .
After I had written this down I suddenly saw the E.B.
and he said, " Be comforted, my son, for the day is not
very far hence when you will rejoice that you are unable
to do as other men. (This prediction came true in the
end). I can not stay with you now, but I will come to
you and your tutor on Sunday evening. My blessing
be with you." Then he smiled and went away. Now I
feel better. I was longing to see the E.B. again, it seems
so long since he has been. Last night while I was
cogitating in bed, I saw a spirit with a lovely aura but a
queer kind of face a bit like a Chinese doll but much
nicer. He stood at the foot of my bed and smiled ever
so sweetly but said nothing. I wonder who he is and
what he wanted? I have a feeling he'll come again.
Fluffy seems much preoccupied with her two kittens,
which she washes a great deal. How awful it would be
if women had to lick their babies all over like that. Mrs.
Webster called on the P's this afternoon for tea, and her
aura was all grey. (A sign of depression). I was in one
of my knowing (psychic) moods, and got that she was
moping because her husband didn't love her properly
and she thought he was mashed on some other lady, or
perhaps she wasn't even a lady. Any how when she
had cleared out, I told the P's what I thought, and they
were mighty surprised and sort of made a face at each
other and Mr. P. said, half laughing, " You're too sharp,
my lad, there's no hiding anything from *you*." And so
I knew I was right. But of course I wouldn't say anything like that to any one else, not me.

Sept. 26.

The E.B. came to see us yesterday, and afterwards

that nice spirit with the queer face (Thibetan features) who I saw (while) in bed. This is what Mr. P. wrote down.

(The E.B.) "Greetings, my sons. I have come to you to-day because there are several things I would say to you. Each soul who is consciously treading the path of Spiritual Knowledge has two Teachers. You, my younger son, have already seen your other Teacher, though as yet he has not spoken to you, but will do so presently. He occupies a Thibetan body, and you may think of him as "The Lama", for his name need not be disclosed. Perhaps you wonder why it is necessary for each pupil who is striving towards the Light to have two Masters? Yet were I to explain this to you now, you would not understand. Therefore let it suffice that it *is* so, and that in the meantime you take it on faith until the day dawns when we may dare to give out more knowledge. Love us both, my sons; not because we demand love for ourselves, but because love is a force which we can use for good. Love is also a bridge which spans the unseen. On the wings of love, your mind may fly to us in its bewilderment and receive its answer . . . . You have wondered my beloved son, why it is so long since I have appeared to you. But realise we too are governed by natural laws, and it is not always possible to come when your heart desires our presence. Nevertheless, our voices may be heard by those who know how to listen. And so, when there is a problem that frets you, think of us forcibly with love, then still the ripples of your mind and listen with your inner self, and you will receive the answer. But ask not questions which are prompted by idle curiosity, for those we must not

197

answer—and it is doubtful whether they would even reach us . . . . And now here is my Brother who would speak to you. Farewell."

(The Lama). "I greet you, my brothers, who know me not in the flesh, yet know me in the spirit. To-day it shall be my joy and privilege to recall to your memories those three great truths which ye have learned in the past but have not brought over into your present rebirths. Bear with me if I am brief, I have not the same command of your mother-tongue which my Brother evinces. Peradventure before long it will be possible to commune in thought only, leaving my mouthpiece to clothe it in his own words. But that time is not yet. Know, my brothers:

There is but one LIFE manifesting through all forms.
There is but one SELF manifesting through all selves.
There is but one LOVE manifesting through all loves.

The SELF is one with LIFE and the SELF is one with LOVE, therefore are the three but one. He who realises his unity with the LIFE, SELF and LOVE knoweth Bliss, for pure LIFE is Bliss, the pure SELF is Bliss, and pure (unconditional) LOVE is Bliss. When the sun shines through crimson glass there appears to be a crimson sun, and when the sun shines through emerald glass there appears to be an emerald sun, yet is there but one sun which is neither crimson nor emerald. And so it is with the one SELF shining through a myriad individual selves, which are as but the coloured windows through which the sun of the SELF doth shine. These truths which I have enunciated are the great Simples, yet are they the eternal profundities. Ponder

198

on them. And I beseech the elder of you to elucidate them to the younger, for it is meet he should already absorb them in the morning of his incarnation. Peace be with you. I go, yet will I return."

When the Lama had gone, Mr. Patmore scratched his head and said, " That'll take a bit of thinking over." But to-day he explained it to me, and I think I understand it just a bit.

Sept. 30.

The Lama came again yesterday and asked us if we had thought about what he said. And so we told him we had. Then he said: " My brothers, perceive the one SELF in all beings, then will ye love all beings. In your scriptures it is written ' love they neighbour as thyself ', and ye have deemed that to mean, love thy neighbour as much as thyself. But ye err, for it also means thou shouldst love thy neighbour as thyself because he is one with thyself, seeing there is but one SELF. Verily there are many waves in the sea, yet are those waves one with the sea and formed out of the sea, and their difference is not of kind but only of name and form. And so it is with thyself and thy neighbours. Only when Mankind shall realise this will all enmities cease. Not facts but illusions are the causes of discord in the world. The mother of conflict is the illusion of diversity; the mother of unhappiness is the search *without* for that which is *within.* Every soul, whether wittingly or unwittingly, is striving to find the bliss of the SELF; the sage tries to find it through wisdom and saintliness and the sinner through folly and sinfulness; the desire is the same but the methods are

199

diverse. Blame not the sinner, my brothers, but have compassion on him, for his sinfulness is but ignorance, incurring none the less its retribution, be it in the present or the future. This is what we of the East call the law of karma, but you of the West have erased its truth from your religion, deeming that a man can evade the consequences of his misdeeds through repentance. Yet is the law of karma a benignant law, for if man could elude the consequences of searching for the SELF in the wrong way, how would he ever come to think to search for it in the right way? Through the ways of error doth man ultimately arrive at Truth—the Truth of the SELF which shall set him free. Peace be with you."

I asked Mr. Patmore why our second teacher was called after an animal? And he said he wasn't, and that the animal was spelt with two L's, but when it had only one L it meant a sort of monk.

Mr. P. remarked that he envied me being able to see such high spirits, and wished to goodness *he* could see and hear them. Poor Mr. P.—it must be very irksome to be half blind . . . . Bridget has got a drastic cold and sneezes all over the house. I suppose I shall be the next.

Oct. 11.

On Saturday we went to Harrogate for the day to see a Mr. Kelly who is a friend of Mr. P's, and had luncheon with him. Mr. P. really wanted to pay a visit to a fortune teller (clairvoyante and medium) who he had heard of, and wanted to take me with him to see what I could see. So after luncheon we toddled along and it was great fun. Madam Stick-in-the-Mud was quite a decent old thing with a fairly nice aura. She told me I had very high influences around me, or some such word, and she didn't often meet people like us who were so spiritual, and had such beautiful auras. She wanted to know who she was to do first, and Mr. P. told her to start on me. Whereupon she looked into a glass ball (a crystal) she had, and began to tell my fortune.

She said I'd be a great painter and go and journey across water, and that I'd get married rather young and be very happy. But she said I'd have to be careful about my health as I wasn't at all strong. She told me I was very clairvoyant and would be able to see things when I got older and would (also) have the gift of healing and be able to cure people by laying on of hands, and that I'd do a lot of good. She did pile it on, I must say, and I wondered what she was up to. She said I'd be very rich, and would make a lot of money with my pictures too. (Quite wrong; I never sold a picture in my life. As to my first marriage—she did not foresee my second one—it was by no means a happy alliance. Altogether I think her prognostications were a mixture of psychism and guess-work, like that of so many professional fortune-tellers.) After she had told me all this, she asked us if we'd like her guide to speak to us, and Mr. P. said we would. While she was talking I had seen a queer looking spirit hanging about dressed up like those Red Indians I have seen in my picture books, but I didn't know what he wanted. When we said we'd like to speak to her guide, she pulled the curtains a bit to darken the room, and then sat down and shut her eyes. Then she began to wriggle and go on in a rum way which made me feel quite uncomfortable, and made me think she was going to have a fit.

Suddenly the spirit disappeared inside her and began to speak very queer, (i.e. in broken English) so as I could hardly tell what he was talking about. He sort of talked like a little child, and made me want to giggle. I can't for the life of me remember all he said, and Mr. P. couldn't see in the dark to take it down. But he seemed to pay us a lot of blarney (compliments) and made out we were great swells because we believed in spiritualism and all that. He said there wasn't much difference between sleeping and dying, and that after a manner of speaking we die every night when we fall asleep, because we leave our bodies. The only thing is we come back to them in the morning, but when we really die, we *don't*, and that is all there is to it. When it was time for him to clear off, he said, " Me must go now. Me was very glad to speak with you. Me hope you will come again." After that I saw him coming out of Madam Thingumybob. But there was another spirit there who tried to get into her (take control) but didn't seem to manage it properly, and sort of hung about outside her and tried to make her talk to Mr. P. He said he was Uncle Jim, which surprised Mr. P. very much. Then I heard him say a lot of things, but when they came out of the old gal's mouth they weren't the same what he'd said, and sounded all silly, because she'd got them all mixed up somehow, I don't know why. (14)

After this had gone on for a bit, he said he'd have to say good-bye as the power was giving out, or some such words. And then off he went, and soon afterwards she opened her eyes. Poor Mr. P. didn't get much of his fortune told, because then she said she was too tired to do any more that time, and hoped he'd come again some other day. And that was he end of that. After Mr. P. had paid her something for her trouble, we moved on.

There was just time to go and see Auntie Maud before our train went back home. So we paid her a surprise visit, and she was ever so nice and made herself very pleasant to Mr. P. over tea. Of course we didn't tell her what we'd been up to, but said we'd been spending the day with Mr. Kelly. We had the carriage to ourselves in the train, and I told Mr. P. all I'd seen, and that his uncle had a bald head and side whiskers, which he said was right enough, but that he seemed to have lost his brains since he'd become a spirit. So I told him that was Madam Stickinthemud's fault and not his, because she made a muddle of nearly everything he said. I asked Mr. P. why she called herself madam when she wasn't French? And he replied that that was just a little habit such people had, though he thought it very silly. It was dark when we got home, and Mrs. P. was all agog to hear about the whole concern.

Oct. 20.

Grandpa came to-day, and told us he was soon going into a higher world (on to a higher plane) and it wouldn't be so easy for him to turn up and talk to us then. I might still be able to see him, but he wasn't certain. Well, I hope I can. It would be a great calamity if I couldn't see dear old grandpa any more.

* * * *

A ND here, as far as the reader is concerned the diary comes to an abrupt ending. Having, some years later, taken the copy-books containing the second sections of the diary to the Italian Lakes—this by way of entertaining his first wife—the author had the misfortune to leave them in the train; and as Italy in those days was not especially noted for the honesty of its populace, he never succeeded in recovering them, the reason presumably being that they were in a piece of luggage containing other effects. I understand from his widow who, as already implied, had been his second wife, that the lost sections of the diary brought it up to his twentieth year, after which period, his diary-keeping habits became of a so highly sporadic nature that they could hardly be termed keeping a diary at all. It seems that he would merely jot down a few thoughts and impressions in various notebooks, the outward appearance of which was so insignificant that in the process of house-moving they were disposed of as waste paper. Had he been married at the time to his second wife, this catastrophe would doubtless have been prevented; but as his first wife had developed an extreme aversion to his psychic faculties and his preoccupation with the occult and everything connected with it, she was probably glad of the opportunity to dispose of his papers in so convenient and unobtrusive a manner. It must be conceded, however, that the untidy habits of the diarist himself and his complete indifference to the more mundane features of everyday existence were partly to blame for this. For, as Mrs X. informed me, rather than give himself the trouble of sorting out his papers when their accumulation had become too formidable for comfort, he would nonchalantly request her to make a bonfire of the entire collection, and leave him in undisturbed peace to pursue whatever occupation he happened to be engaged in at the moment.

This brings me to the writing of a brief outline of his life (as related to me by his widow) after he had left the benevolent care of the enlightened and lovable Mr. Patmore, who, it may be stated *en passant*, lived to a ripe old age, and then passed peacefully into the Beyond while dosing in his chair; his amiable and unassuming wife having preceded him by only a few months.

When eighteen years of age the diarist was taken by his parents to Germany and placed with a family living in Wiesbaden. The object was a threefold one; that he should become well-acquainted with the German language, that he should undergo treatment at the hands of German doctors, and finally, at his own request, that he should continue his musical studies in "the home of music."

Having remained a few years in the comparatively salubrious climate of Wiesbaden—albeit with occasional visits to London—he discovered that despite his intense love of music, his talents tended more in the direction of painting, and he therefore resolved to go to Paris for the purpose of studying Art. And though his puritanical mother raised objections to this project on the grounds that the French Capital was "a frivolous and depraved city" whose denizens were addicted to Sabbath-breaking and other manifestations of ungodliness, her protests were not allowed to carry weight with her son, who had not only attained his majority but also had inherited a substantial sum of money, which, to say the least, would keep the proverbial wolf a very safe distance from the door. Moreover his father favoured the project because his son would thereby acquire a certain desirable proficiency in the language of culture and refinement.

It was in the Parisian *pension* where he boarded that he met the beautiful American girl who was afterwards destined to become his first wife, but who at the time was endeavouring unsuccessfully to develop a not-too-remarkable voice under the tuition of one of the many renowned singing-teachers who in those days flourished in Paris. Being in the circumstances fated to meet with a frequency calculated to inflame the romantic passions, the hearts of the two young people became inextricably entangled, and about eighteen months later they were married in London with the due pomp and circumstance which so often attends such functions After a honeymoon on the Rhine, they settled down to conjugal existence in a house in London.

But unfortunately in the course of time the rose-coloured happiness of the first few months began perceptibly to fade; and it soon became apparent to both parties that, instead of having married a complement, they had each married an opposite without any of those enlivening advantages which a contrast is said to present. The young Mrs. X. displayed ambitions and inclinations to reach the highest steps of the social staircase, whilst her husband had a marked aversion to such rarified emptinesses. There were other elements which created disharmony between the couple. His wife seems to have been somewhat strongly sexed, whereas he himself was not overtroubled by immoderate sexual desires. But the most disrupting feature of their married life was his wife's jealousy over his preoccupation with those interests and activities in which she could not share; his painting for one, but more especially his Occultism and its concomitants, both of which deflected his attention from her captivating though egotistical self. In addition to all this, she had to contend with his unpunctuality, his disconcerting forgetfulness that the inner man requires to be sustained at set times of the day, and that even the master of the house cannot demand meals at the most unseasonable hours without deranging the equilibrium of the whole household.

One is tempted to wonder why a man with such pronounced psychic faculties should not have been able to size up his wife's character prior to marrying her, and also to get a premonition that the marriage would not prove a success. But here we are confronted with one of those strange ironies of the psychic temperament. Only the highest Adepts can foretell their own destinies. Indeed, clairvoyance of the predictive type is so subtle a matter that it is almost impossible to exclude the element of wishful thinking in connection with any prophesy which concerns the clairvoyant himself. As to the diarist's failure to size up his fiancée's character from her aura, one must remember that a state of in-loveness materially, if transiently, alters the auric emanations, and that even normally selfish persons become to a large extent unselfish when all their thoughts are centred on another being.

But to return to the main issue. The highly inauspicious alliance endured for some nine years, and was then abruptly ended by a tragic and unsuccessful attempt to bring a child into the world when its mother was seemingly unfit for such an undertaking. Judging from one of his letters and from what I have learnt from the second Mrs. X., the diarist had a premonition (which in this instance proved correct) that the child would be stillborn and its mother's life endangered; but as she was so intent on having a child and the doctors thought it would prove beneficial to her health and happiness, he was overruled, and she died in her thirtieth year.

Meanwhile, about seven years after his marriage, the diarist had met the much more sympathetic and understanding Scottish girl who was destined to become his second wife. In fact, owing to the close friendship which was cemented between them, his letters to her became at times so frequent and lengthy as almost to constitute a diary in themselves. But unfortunately with that careless and unbusinesslike indifference to detail which characterised his manhood, most of the letters are undated, only the day of the week being mentioned. Many of these epistles were penned while their writer was travelling abroad unaccompanied by his neurotic wife, who complained that travelling was too fatiguing to be altogether enjoyable. Whether the reason she gave was a valid one or not is of no importance. In any event, her husband appears to have made somewhat frequent journeys to the Continent, and it is the extracts from his "travel-letters" which constitute the remainder of this volume, together with one or two memorandums which the second Mrs. X. contrived to rescue from the fate of being consigned to the rubbish heap. Apart from a few sentences here and there, most of the chosen extracts are concerned with psychic matters and philosophical reflections.   (C.S.)

WRITTEN IN A NOTE-BOOK, APPARENTLY DURING THE EARLY YEARS OF THE FIRST MARRIAGE OF THE DIARIST.

Undated.

It is getting pretty obvious that our marriage is a hopeless failure. I have never complained to the E.B. before, but when, after my meditation to-day he suddenly appeared, I am rather ashamed to say I let myself go a bit. Why hadn't he warned me that I wasn't the right person to make J. happy? I confess his answer made me feel a little sheepish. He said in effect: " We Elder Brothers do not exist for the purpose of cicumventing the karma of our pupils. Both you and your wife have certain karma to work off together, and had I warned you, I would have been frustrating the designs of the Lords of Karma. This is of course never permitted. My son, you have made your bed, you must lie upon it. Why do you suppose that until they have passed the 5th Initiation clairvoyants, except on rare occasions, are not allowed to foresee their own destinies? To be warned would be to be forearmed. I have answered you. Blessings, my son . . ." After that he smiled and departed.

Letter written to Miss G. (afterwards the second Mrs. **X**.)
. . . . Lovely scenery spoilt by a horrid psychic atmosphere. They must have practised a lot of Black Magic

209

along this coast at one time. Most unpleasant thought-forms left over. Impossible to dissipate them with mediation; might as well light a joss-stick over a cesspool Came through Marseilles yesterday. A sink of depravity. Made an interesting observation. There are some altruistic *devas* on the hills behind the place. They absorb all the filthy psychic miasma from the town into themselves, then throw it out again all purified. (15). Otherwise some horrible catastrophe would overtake Marseilles . . . . Shall have a look round Monte Carlo next week. Write to me *Poste Restante.* . .

Monte Carlo. Thursday.

. . . . What a place Paradise and hell combined! You have no idea what the psychic vibrations are like. I can only stand it for two days, then Italy for me! . . . The *devas* on these hills are different from those at Marseilles: they sort of shrink from the whole business. If it were not for the lot of good music to be heard here (which undoubtedly has to a limited extent a purifying influence) I believe the powers that be would have the Casino burnt down. That will probably happen in the end, or perhaps the place will get submerged. Fire and water are the only lasting purifiers in a case like this. . . .

Florence. Tuesday.

How I love Italy, with its cathedrals and churches and monks and nuns and priests! But they are a libidinous lot, some of them. I was riding in a bus this afternoon. A rather pretty English woman was just about to sit down beside a priest when I saw him quickly put his hand on the seat for her to sit on. Of course she jumped up and glared at him furiously, and he smiled and apologised, pretending it was not intentional. But I could see his unpleasant red aura, and knew otherwise. It would be much better if priests were allowed to marry. Why expect them to be devoid of sexual feelings? After all they are human. I should like to live here. But it is not my karma. I have already had one incarnation in Italy. Was a monk. Got a memory through about it yesterday when I was up at Fiesoli. But it is too long to relate in a letter, or I should say in this letter, when I am feeling rather tired. . . To-day I visited one of the Galleries. Certainly the Xtian religion has been a great inspiration to painters in the past. Yet I have an unwelcome presentiment that its days are numbered and that there won't be many more Popes. Religions come and go. When they have served their purpose they disappear. I think one of the most popular cults of the future will be Spiritualism—that is, when the technique of communication has vastly improved. Of the future of Theosophy I can't be at all certain. The Lama said that two of the Brothers had only tried it more or less as an experiment. I don't mean that I doubt its truth—as far as I know it; but how people will react to it when there is no longer some compelling and forceful personality at its head is another matter. . .

Bellagio (Italian Lakes). Friday.

. . . . I arrived here on Tuesday. I wish you were here with me to enjoy the entrancing beauty of the place " where every prospect pleases " and man is *not* vile, but only pleasant and simple . . . I have been thinking about religion again. Up on the great cliff which over-hangs Caddanabbia is a little chapel. Coming in the train, I don't know how many similar little chapels I didn't see perched up on the summit of hills. That is the sort of decoration I miss on the English hills. The only one I can think of at the moment is St. Martha's Chapel near Guildford. Or is it St. Martin's? I forget. Never mind. What I was about to say is: how much poetry and picturesqueness we should lose in life were it not for religion—of some kind. It is the church steeple or church tower which gives the poetical finish-ing-touch to every village; it is the church bells wafted on the evening breeze which provide poetic music for the soul. Are these things of beauty not going to be " a joy forever "? . . . . I have just heard a voice saying to me: " Be not distressed, my son. We shall always inspire some form of religion to suit the needs of the people. But how can even *we* foretell what pre-cise nature it will take when we do not know how the greater part of mankind will develop morally and spirit-ually during the next few hundred years? So far only comparatively few have begun to put into practice what the Master Christ taught some two thousand years ago. Because of this foolish disregard of moral and spirit-ual laws, Humanity will soon have to be plunged into great tribulation so that it may learn through exper-ience what it refused to learn through wisdom" . . . . That isn't very pleasant news, I must say. Wonder what sort of tribulation it will be? Surely not a war! We may be stupid, but are we quite stupid enough for that after we have just had one war, which I am not at all certain has redounded to our credit? I can say this to *you*, but for a great Empire to set on a small community like the Boers—its real motive being love of money—is like a great hulking man bashing a woman about because he can't induce her to give him what he wants!

. . . . . I have been reading Henry James. If the art of saying very little in as many words as possible constitutes a great writer then H.J. deserves the laurel-wreath. But it seems to me that the only justification for saying a thing in a lengthy way is to say it in an amusing way, and I'm damned if I can see the least humour in H.J. Some of his paragraphs are so cryptic that I suspect they mean something highly indecent.* Personally I think it needs more skill to express an extremely indecent thing in an ultra refined manner than to cover it over with ambiguities à la H.J. The one is usually humorous, the other is merely tedious. Still, who am I to indulge in criticism? My youthful ambi-

---

* The E.B. has just telepathically rebuked me in his tolerant manner for my remark (about indecency). He says there is nothing indecent in Nature; it is merely our wrong attitude towards it which makes us *think* it indecent. This wrong attitude is largely the result of Vanity. There are certain things we regard as undignified, so we hush them up and say they are "not nice." We have still to learn not to be such hypocrites and to look upon Nature with a pure eye . . . How very true. And what a price we English pay for our hypocrisy. In "The Fatherland" prostitutes are periodically examined by the police-doctors; in England we try to pretend that prostitutes don't exist. Result, the spread of venereal disease. We are more syphilised than civilised!

tions to write have faded away like other foolish ambitions . . . . It has just flashed down on me 'psychically" that I was a writer in my last incarnation and I brought over the desire to write in this one. That accounts for my sticking to the diary so long, when other youngsters would have got tired of it. However, I was not meant to be a writer in this life, but to develop and help people a bit with my psychism, and also to a certain extent with my paintings. Apropos of my expired literary ambitions, I sense that when people get a violent if temporary craze for say, writing poetry, composing music or painting pictures at one time or other of their lives, it is simply because they have done these things in a former life. But why the desire should crop up at a given moment, I don't pretend to account for—it may have to do with the astrological aspects. I shall make a meditation about this one day . . . . I find it very difficult to get sufficient sleep in this small village. First of all the church clock chimes very loudly every quarter of an hour, and in addition, these sonorous-voiced Italians seem to have violent altercations just below my window till the dawn is in the sky. In point of fact they are merely conversing! . . . .

Lugano. Saturday.

. . . . Have just had a long letter from J. (his wife) full of complainings. She wants me back again. But when I do go back there will only be scenes. I am that sort of a husband that J. likes when I'm absent, and dislikes when I'm present. As I can't be absent and present at the same time there is no cure for such a situation. Still—there it is. Although I don't want to

214

return to London and leave my beloved Italy, there are compensations; one of them will be to see *you* again. Besides, there are more people needing treatment. Another thing: A— has got several documents for me to sign. How all that does bore me. I believe that if I had to make money, I should live in a hovel rather than waste my time trying to accumulate the shekels. Which reminds me, I never answered your question about that picture of mine your friend wants to buy. She can have it with pleasure. But not for money. I have made up my mind that I shall never *sell* a picture. (I will fish it out for her when I get home). I paint for love and not for filthy lucre. That is my return for the affluent circumstances in which I am placed   Rather amusing; the Lama turned up suddenly after I had written that sentence, and said " You would not be in those circumstances if you had not earned them by your great generosity in a previous incarnation   That is the deeper significance of the text in your Scriptures: As a man sows so shall he reap." He then went on to say that every true artist is, without knowing it, a sort of *Karma Yogi*, because he works for work's sake without bothering about the reward . . . There is a man in this hotel with that awful disease called, I think, disseminated sclerosis. I asked the Lama what sort of misdeeds in a past life produced such a frightful condition? And he said, *cruelty*. The man had been an Inquisitor in a previous incarnation. Thank God I have managed to avoid *that* karma! To be born a hunchback is likewise the result of cruelty. But I asked, what is the use of it all if the victims of such self-made karma don't remember? And he said, the physical brain doesn't remember, but the "soul" does . . . There is one thing about these Latin races I don't like, and that is their cruel treatment of animals. Yet looking at their auras, they are not really cruel, they merely lack a particular kind of imagination. That of course would make all the difference to the resultant karma. One thing has always puzzled me, however. It doesn't seem a very benignant ruling of the Deity that animals themselves should be born with the instinct to prey on one another. But the Lama said, how otherwise would they evolve? By this means they learn a certain amount of cunning which helps to develop their faculties. Animals are not cruel in the sense that some men are cruel, because they are not conscious of cruelty *as such*. The cat who plays with a mouse is just as happy playing with a reel of cotton . . . . I had never thought of that . . . . There is an Italian girl here who is meltingly beautiful, and made me feel quite sentimental until I heard her voice. That is the trouble; so many of these women have voices almost like fog-horns Some of the men are most picturesque and others look like murderers, but are quite harmless.

Extracts from letters written in the following year.

Paris. Monday.

. . . . It is enjoyable being with all my old artist friends again. But I am finding the aura of this city of "pissoirs and prostitutes" rather disturbing in my present mood, and have decided to start for Spain already next week. Write to me *Poste restante* Toledo . . . I foresee a time when painting will become more and more suggestive of the "lower levels" of the astral plane.

What with its muddy colours and one thing and another it is distinctly heading in that direction. The phase will probably last about sixty years, and then there will be a reaction. Most of these friends of mine think my pictures completely mad. Perhaps they are, but not to me. I paint a poor reflection of the sort of things I see in my visions of the higher planes. That doesn't appeal to men who think there is only one plane—the material..

Toledo. Friday.

. . . . I'm tormented by fleas here. It really is disgusting. I spend half the time scratching myself. And yet this is supposed to be a decent hotel . . . . The Spanish landscape is rather disappointing in some ways. One thinks of Spain as a feast of colour, but the rocky regions are all sombre-coloured and austere . . . I have always suspected that in one of my incarnations I came up against the Inquisition, and this afternoon I got a *memory* confirming it. The atmosphere of the place must have brought it back. One hears a lot about the unfortunates who were burnt at the stake or suffered the tortures of the rack, but one seldom hears of those who retracted their "heresy" and got off with a few minor penances. Well, unless my vision was askew, I was one of the latter. Being suspected of heretical notions, which undoubtedly I possessed, I was brought before the tribunal. Some of the men were a nasty looking lot, but not all of them. One or two really believed they were saving souls in this fantastic and excruciating manner. Others may also have believed it, but they had a lustful relish for cruelty as well, however unconscious it may have been. My attitude towards the

217

whole business seems to have differed considerably from those martyrs who apparently and perhaps rather arrogantly took their own convictions so seriously that they were ready to die for them.

In fact I have long since decided that most of the martyrs merely had a taste for self-advertisement; in short, the desire for martyrdom was actuated by a subtle form of vanity. They did not realise it themselves, but come to that, who realises *any*thing about himself? The E.B. says, by the way, that in the not distant future there will be a whole science "put through" concerned with self-realisation . . . . But I am digressing. As my own beliefs in those days were of a secret character and not suited for the world in general, it would have been a sheer waste of martyrdom for me to have gone to the stake, or even suffered the "lesser" form of "unpleasantness!" The way out of the difficulty was quite simple. I argued that these men with their absurd assumptions that there was only one approach to God, viz: through the 'Holy Church," were little better—or rather much worse—than children, and therefore the simplest thing to do was to humour them just as one humours little lads and lasses who believe puerile nonsense of some form or other. Why should I pay these silly fools the compliment of being honest with them when they themselves were treating me to a montsrous lie? And so I pretended that I had been entirely won over by their impressive arguments, and henceforth would renounce any heretical notions I may have once possessed. Being a vain and fanatical lot, this flattered their vanity of course, and the penances I had to undergo for having ever doubted the Church were comparatively light. Please don't think I want to blow my own trumpet—especially as some people would, perhaps rightly say I had been a coward—but I think it was my fortunate lack of conceit which saved my skin. For I do consider it a form of conceit when a person imagines he holds the absolute truth, and is so convinced of this that he is ready to be burnt alive or have all his limbs dislocated for the rest of his earthly life. And what a naive conception of the Deity! Would God be so small-minded as to worry in what form He was approached? But the besetting sin of the Church throughout its entire history has been its *love of power*. And even in those days I seem to have appreciated this fact.

Another point, though I find it a bit difficult to put it into the right words: I mean that if one disbelieves a thing sufficiently, one isn't afraid to pretend one believes it. Are you afraid to pretend at Christmas time, for the sake of your little niece, that you believe in Santa Claus? No. Because you know perfectly well that it is a matter of supreme indifference to Santa Claus (I suppose he was a person?) whether you believe in him or not. Enough of this. I will write again in a few days if there is anything worth relating . . . .

Madrid. Wednesday.

. . . . I have had a letter from my wife telling me she is pregnant. The news worries me. As I told you, I have always had a presentiment that it would not be good for J. to have a child, but I allowed myself to be persuaded by the doctors. When I asked the E.B. about it, he was non-committal, and told me that the man who

219

never took any risks in life would get nowhere. This is quite true, of course. But all the same, I am not very happy about the whole business . . . . I met a monk here yesterday, and to my astonishment discovered he was an Englishman. This struck me as so curious that I began to size him up psychically. What I got was this: he is one of those lazy souls, (and I use the word soul in its literal sense) who is wasting his incarnation and simply repeating the experiences of his last life. If he had done his duty, he ought to have been an active business-man taking part in the affairs of men. But he hankered so much after the peace and quiet of his last incarnation, when he was a Franciscan monk, that he couldn't resist the temptation to withdraw from the world again. Naturally he doesn't know all this, and I couldn't very well tell him, for he certainly wouldn't have believed me, and probably would have thought I was an emissary from his lordship the Devil! The Lama turned up this evening and told me I had been quite right about the monk, and that there were quite a number of indolent souls who shirked their duties in the same way. But they get no satisfaction out of the choice they have made, because nearly all the time they are conscious of a sort of conflict going on inside themselves for which they cannot account. This would explain why I could see from the man's aura that he was not really happy. Rather interesting, isn't it?

Madrid. Sunday.

I went to High Mass here to-day to see what I could sense. There is certainly a form, somewhat like an Eastern temple, built up in rarefied substance during

220

the ceremony, and when the Host is elevated, a large *Deva* is invoked which sheds its radiance over the whole assembly. All very beautiful for those who can *see*. But how much the worshippers get out of it depends a good deal on their power to respond. Some of the auras around me were noticeably affected in a beneficial way, others much less so . . . . In view of what J. has written me about her "interesting condition," I have decided to come home sooner than I intended. Hope to see you in about a week . . . .

Extracts from Letters Written after the Death of the first Mrs. X.

London. Monday.

. . . . I get from your thoughts that float my way that you are quite enjoying your sojourn! in the country. Am I right? . . . . L. and F. (two mutual friends) have fallen violently in love and are determined to get married. I can see from their auras, which don't really harmonise, that their marriage won't be a success. I warned L. but she refuses to believe me; so obviously it is their karma to get spliced and to rue it afterwards. I'm sorry, but what can one do? I even went so far as to tell the girl that she had better be P's mistress rather than tie herself up. Needless to say, she was merely horrified at me for giving her such scandalous advice! Yet I'm pretty certain of this—if they would live together for a time, they *would* soon find their state of romantic intoxication would wear off, and that they were not true mates. I've come to the conclusion that when *some* people are in love, they contact each other's higher self or soul, and are blind to the "personality" i.e.

221

the subtler bodies which are temporarily purified through the uplifting vibrations of in-love-ness. You understand what I mean? It is rather difficult to put into words. I don't require to tell *you* that the whole thing is karmic when people get blinded in that sort of way, (just as J. and I were), and not realising it, go and link themselves up for life. You may say: then why did I try to prevent L. and F. making fools of themselves? But you might as well ask why attempt to rescue a drowning man? The obvious answer is: if you can save him, it is his karma to be saved, and if you can't, then it is his karma to be drowned. I hope I'm .wrong about L. and F. but I'm afraid I'm right. *(My husband's prediction turned out to be correct).*

Keswick. Sunday. (Written a few months after his first wife's death).

. . . . Please send some prayerful thoughts to J. as I am doing myself. She is not happy yet on the " astral plane " and can't acclimatise herself to a life in which Society in the worldly sense plays no part! I was told this by the mater who has contacted her. *(My husband's mother passed over a few years after his first marriage).* J. rather stubbornly keeps away from me because she resented my interest in psychic matters while she was on earth, as you know. The mater is very different, and seems to enjoy turning up for a little " talk " now and then . . . . It's quite like old times being with my old tutor again, and he is remarkably energetic considering his age. He can walk further than I can without getting tired. What a nuisance this groggy heart of mine is, especially when I should like to be climbing

222

the hills which look so lovely in their vernal garb. I wish you could be with us.

We had a regular "sitting" last night, and the old man took down a lot of stuff in shorthand. The E.B. told us that J. had passed over in that sudden and tragic manner as the karmic result of infanticide in a previous incarnation. So it seems that I was an indirect instrument of the Lords of Karma The thought is not a very pleasant one. But as the E.B. said, with his wonderful smile: if it hadn't been me, it would have had to be some one else . . . . I enclose a few of the utterances the dear old chap has copied from his short-hand notes. If you are interested enough to copy them out, do so, but please return the original as Mr.——* wants to add them to his collection.

The E. B. said :

"My sons, I rejoice to be able to speak to you both again in this atmosphere of brotherly love and harmony. A while ago, one of my Brothers told *you,* my younger son, of the great tribulation that ere long mankind is destined to suffer; this in preparation for a new Age which shall dawn, and which is foretold in your Scriptures. Roughly speaking, the end of the present Age will come to pass in about forty years, and its death-pangs and the birth-pangs of the new Age will be attended with much agony of soul and body for the un-enlightened . . . . These pangs could have been avoided if humanity had but harkened to the voice of the Sages and attempted not to try and rule the world by the dictates of selfishness, dishonesty, mendacity and the employment of force. But what has been, cannot now at this late hour be altered, and the karma that Man has sown must 'ere long be reaped in all its painfulness. I tell you this, my sons, not to alarm you, but to prepare you for the making of a decision over which I shall ask you to ponder. When the great travail shall come and the world shall be plunged in darkness, then we Initiates—or rather some of us—of the Right-Hand Path who constitute the Great White Lodge, as it is called, must consider taking new bodies —Western ones—and leaving the comparative seclusion of our present habitations, so that we may walk more freely among men, and assist, so to speak, in a more material way in the difficult task of reconstruction.

We shall desire to gather round us many of our pupils, who will then be in personal contact with us on the physical plane, and not merely contact us in the spirit, as heretofore. But this, in your case, my sons, will demand a certain sacrifice; a curtailment of your sojourn, between your incarnations, on what we may loosely term the celestial Realms. For it means that after you have shed your present bodies, you must return to the troubles and limitations of earthly existence far sooner than you may wish. For this reason, I ask you to ponder over this sacrifice now while you are still on earth. Remember that we Elder Brothers never command or impel, we merely suggest; and whether our suggestions are acted upon or disregarded may often have much to do with our future decisions. Verily, my sons, we also have our problems, and although we are beyond sorrow and suffering as *ye* know them, it often taxes our ingenuity to the utmost how best to guide and help the multitude of heedless and unruly children who constitute present-day humanity: therefore do we need the aid of our pupils who have the same aspirations but as yet not the same powers. . . . Nor is this all. We and our more advanced pupils will require to master new magnetic currents which will come into play at the end of the Age when a new Cosmic Force will be precipitated on to the earth's aura from higher spheres " . . . .

The E.B. then went on to tell us something about the effects of this new Force, but requested me not to commit the information to paper. Afterwards he asked us if we wanted to put any questions. After telling him we would of course do what he had previously begged of us, I put the question:

" Why can't you come among men in your present bodies? Why must you take new ones? "

" Because those we occupy at the present," he said, " are not suited for such a purpose, being too sensitive to withstand the coarse vibrations of the mundane world. They have served us in the present Age under the conditions in which we live, and will continue to serve us a while longer; but in the coming Age we shall need to adjust ourselves to the altered circumstances and to the forward step in evolution. All, my sons, is in process of *becoming*. Nothing is static in the manifested Universe, and even the Solar Spirit has not reached final perfection and must go through further Initiations before this Solar System goes into latency, and we shall rest, as your Scriptures say, " in the bosom of the Father" . . . . And now I must depart. But my Brother, who is here, would speak to you a few words."

The Lama.

"I greet you, my brothers; though what I would say more especially concerns our younger servitor. Conserve your health during the coming years, my brother. For when the great tribulation approaches you will have important work to accomplish. Lament not over your bodily affliction. One day you will be exceeding glad and come to view it in the light of a blessing. Ask me not why? You will know when the hour shall strike . . . . And you, my older brother, we are pleased with the work you are doing in our service, and the enlightenment you seek to bring to those in darkness. Be not discouraged when you opine that some of them do not respond, for your work shall none the less bear its ultimate fruit in a manner you wot not of. I must not tarry now. Farewell."

Dolgelly. Tuesday.

. . . . The atmosphere of Wales is conducive to bringing through memories of the past, especially if connected with Wales itself. I got that in one life I was a Welsh bard of sorts. That would partly account for my love of music in this incarnation, and an unusual fondness for the harp which musicians rather despise except in the orchestra. Well, I admit that its upper notes do sound rather "tooth-picky," but the kind of harp I used in those days was a smaller and greatly different affair to the cumbersome modern instrument, which I should not care to lug about from place to place That incarnation was not without its excitements. I seem to have been a somewhat outspoken minstrel, and couldn't refrain from having a " dig " now

226

and then at one or other of the chieftains, if chiefs they were, for I only see the thing more or less in pictures. One of the wives of these imposing gentlemen (I don't mean they had more than one wife) appears to have developed amorous feelings towards me and aroused the jealousy of her husband, who took his revenge by having me " put away ". I'll tell you more about it when I see you next . . . . There is a woman staying in the hotel who tipples. She is obsessed by a drunkard of a brother, who got run over while in a state of intoxication. Wanting to test the accuracy of my sensings, I brought the conversation round to "second sight," and asked her if she believed in it. As her answer was in the affirmative, though she admitted she knew very little about it, I asked her if she once had a brother who met with a fatal accident. She was much surprised at this, and said yes. After that, she wanted to know what else I could tell her. (How people do love having their fortunes told!) Could I see into the future? I asked what in particular she wanted to know. Then she treated me to a long rigmarole, half truth and half lies, in which she made out that she had an unkind husband (I could see from her aura that she was deceiving me) and that in consequence she had got very fond of another man (quite true) who didn't reciprocate her feelings to the extent that she might wish, or *pretended* not to, because she was married. Would everything come right in the end? This placed me in a quandary. I could hardly tell her that she'd made herself so repulsive-looking with her bibulous habits that no one would wish to touch her with a barge pole. Nor could I tell her that she looked a bit long in the tooth for evoking

227

amorous sentiments in the opposite sex! As a matter of fact I think she is only about forty-four, but all the drinking has distended her pores and enlarged her features so she looks much older. Besides which, alcohol has obviously loosened her conversational faculties and she hardly ever stops talking from sunrise to sunset. Men don't like over-loquacious women who say *nothing* in a thousand and one different ways! Being egotists, they like women who listen and throw in an occasional remark now and then! All the same, I got that her husband, who still has the remnants of an affection for her, is trying to be patient and put up with her failings, whereas the other man is just using her as a sort of hotel-proprietress to give him a good dinner with plenty of drinks, and fuss around him in a way which pleases his vanity. A not very helpful finding to console a poor woman with—what? No—so I really didn't know what to say. Fortunately the "gods" arranged that some other guests should come into the room when I was struggling with my dilemma, and that put an end to the "sitting." The good lady departs to-morrow, I'm thankful to say. Meanwhile I shall avoid being left *tête-à-tête* with her, since I can do nothing but admonish her to keep her elbow unlifted! And a lot of good that would do. My incorrigible sense of humour may make me sound rather flippant but *you* know that at heart I feel an overwhelming pity for such people . . . .

Which reminds me I had a letter from Mrs. B——, California, who writes that there is a doctor out there who is getting rid of obsessing entities by giving them electric shocks. (16) Now that's very interesting. I am writing her to send me more particulars . . . . I spent the morning in a secluded spot looking at the nature-spirits at work. There are plenty of them to be seen here . . . .

Extracts from a few letters written during the war of 1914 — 1918, and afterwards.

. . . .Yes I miss you too. But I am sure it is better for you to be out of London and with your parents for a while. I will join you for a short visit in a few weeks, but meanwhile be philosophical and keep a stiff upper lip as I have to do with this insanity and misery all around. What enrages me about the whole damn business is not so much its wickedness as its fantastic stupidity. Are we civilised or are we barbarians? The other day a whole lot of school-children were killed by a bomb. Is that a method of settling a dispute? And to think that if I hadn't this groggy heart of mine I should be conscripted before long to stick a bayonet into some German fellow's tummy who is only doing his duty as our own soldiers are doing theirs.* The "righteous indignationists" who sit in their armchairs and curse and swear at the Germans don't realise that, or don't want to. They go on as if every single boche in the whole of the Fatherland was a blood-thirsty England-hating murderer who would like to see every Jack one of us wiped off the surface of the earth! When I mildly

* (Note by Mrs. X. Sorting out my papers. I have just seen what The Lama said some time ago; how my husband would be glad about his heart-trouble one day. I suppose that is what he meant). See *ante*, letter from Keswick.

suggest that that is not the least likely to be true (having stayed in Germany and made many friends there) they think I'm pro-German or a "despicable pacifist" or something of the sort. Looked at from one point of view, the whole war is a wonderful test for the Christian nations. Now we can see who amongst us are capable of loving their enemies when they have got some enemies *to* love Not that there would ever have been a war at all if we were really Christian nations; but that is another matter. And to think that the match that set the whole "bonfire" alight was simply Austria's vanity or *amour propre* if one prefers the euphemism . . . .

London. Thursday.

. . . . I have been too busy and too tired to write before. There has been a perfect stream of bereaved mothers and disconsolate sweethearts to see me, all of them wanting me to get in touch with their "dead" soldier boys. Thank God I can usually manage this, and they go away comforted—at least, some of them do. The worst of it is that I can't always give them very "good news" about their "loved ones," because naturally a certain percentage of them are extremely annoyed and bewildered to find themselves suddenly precipitated onto the astral plane! But at any rate I can usually convey some convincing message proving that they are *they*, which is some slight consolation to their "left-behind ones " . . . . I saw the E.B. for a few moments last night. He says the Brothers lament over the frightful profiteering that is going on. Instead of these people learning selflessness through this war and working off bad karma, they are making more karma and sowing seeds for future trouble. It is rather disgusting, I must say. While the fighters are going through hell abroad, these profiteers are making things all the more difficult for people at home, and increasing the price of living. In addition to all this, the Government is wasting the public's money in the most outrageous manner. I love humanity, but I'm afraid the longer I live the less I think of human nature. At this rate it will be a precious long time before we can have "heaven on earth" . . . . .

Monday.

. . . . Have just come across a most tragic thing as the result of this war. Yesterday D—— (a mutual friend) rang up in great distress and asked me to pop along and see H—— (her husband). Since he got back from the front he has completely changed towards her and the children, and treats them all as if they were strangers. Apart from that, the whole man seems to have changed—his character and everything. When I looked at him (psychically) I found to my horror that it isn't H— at all; another *ego* is occupying his body—got in when he was shell-shocked. H— was always a rather negative sort of fellow, as you know, and now this is what has happened. The whole thing is so distressing, I didn't know what to tell the poor girl. A nice affair to have a husband who isn't your husband, but a stranger in all but his body! Of course obsession is nothing new to me, but in a case like this it's terribly tragic, and at first I couldn't make up my mind whether to tell her the truth or not. I tried to contact the E.B. for advice, but didn't succeed. The Brothers are so

231

busy these days and not always easy to reach in this turgid atmosphere of misery and "bellicosity." However, in the end I thought it best to tell her the worst! but tried to mitigate the verdict a little by saying perhaps one could succeed in hoofing the usurper out. At any rate I shall have a try when out of my body at night. I got in touch with the real H—, who as you may imagine is not very happy at having his body "pinched" in this disgraceful manner. This is the karma of practising a very doubtful form of magic in a past incarnation . . . . No further news of interest . . . .

Written in a note-book, apparently soon after Peace was signed, 1923.

......It doesn't need any clairvoyance to see that this Peace-treaty is a very dubious affair, and may only lead to further trouble in the end. The only idealist at the Conference was President Wilson whose Fourteen Points were inspired by the Brothers. The E.B. as good as told me so by referring to him as " Our Servant." But I have a strong presentiment that the politicians won't keep to his 14 Points, they'll shuffle out of them somehow. I note that Garvin wrote in his Sunday column that the outcome of the whole business would be revenge, sooner or later. And I'm afraid he is right. The psychic atmosphere doesn't suggest Peace to me. This won't have been " the war to end war " or " to make the world safe for democracy." The League of Nations is a wonderful idea. But I get that it will be exploited and simply become a hotbed of intrigue. Politicians don't turn saints all of a sudden! I shall hand this memo over to my wife to keep, just to see if I'm right. If and when another war does come, I hardly expect I shall be still here.

Friday.

. . . . As you know, Mrs. S—, has been worrying me for a long time to go with her to see Mr.— Well, yesterday we went and had a "sitting". I told her she was not to tell him anything about me, and she promised. The man is half genuine and half a fraud. When he can't see anything much, he just invents the most absurd "psychic compliments." He told Mrs. S— that she had some wonderful occult symbols around her, that she was a very advanced soul and that she'd soon be going through an important initiation. All rubbish. I could see none of the symbols, and as for her being a very advanced soul, she is nothing of the kind. Quite a decent old sort, but that is all one can say. When it came to my turn, he informed me that I had a very psychic aura and that I ought to develop my psychic faculties! ! I laughed inwardly, and Mrs. S— looked a bit uncomfortable. He then told me a few mundane things about myself, which I already knew, and finally started on the "compliment-paying tack." Mentioned that I was in touch with very high entities and had gone in for occultism in former incarnations. He admonished me to take great care of my health, as he could see from a patch in my aura that my heart was not all it should be; but with care I ought to live quite a while yet. Kidneys not too good either. Advised me to drink parsley-water. Can't say it was very illuminating, but the old girl was quite satisfied. Set a thief to catch a thief! As soon as psychism is mixed up with earning a living that is the sort of thing one gets. You know the Latin adage: "No man can be wise at all hours of the day"—well—still less can a man be psychic at all hours of the day; the conditions are not always favourable. I don't of course say that all professional clairvoyants are humbugs, far from it. I have known one or two who have been honest enough to say: "There's nothing around you at the moment," or "I'm not in form. Better come another time when conditions are better" . . . . .

Tuesday.

. . . . Saw an old man at the club to-day who had met Mme. Blavatsky. I asked him what he thought of her? And he said, a wonderful personality, but a thorough old fraud. When I asked him what made him think that, he said she had refused to do any phenomena for his friend and himself, her excuse being that the magnetic currents weren't right, or some such nonsense! But surely that rather went to prove that she wasn't a fraud, I said. If she was just a clever conjurer, she could have regaled you with a little display of legerdemain whether the magnetic currents were in order or not. As it was, she was honest enough to tell you the truth. But he couldn't see it. People are so illogical! For fun, just to take him down a peg and to make him less cock-sure of his own opinions, I told him a few things about himself. As I'd never met him before, he was somewhat surprised at what I got! Perhaps it will give him a little food for reflection! . . . . .

Eastbourne. Thursday.

. . . . . I see old President Wilson died. And a disappointed man too. They never stuck to his Fourteen Points, and I believe sorrow hastened his departure. A fine soul much misunderstood. He was used by the Brothers, although I daresay in his physical body he never even heard of them. But he contacted them on the higher planes when out of his body at night. I saw him once or twice over there during the war when I was out of my own body . . . .

London. Monday.

. . . . . I hope you are still enjoying your stay with the F's . . . You will be sorry to hear that my dear old tutor has passed over. He came to see me last night, so I knew he had gone even before the news was confirmed. His wife came with him. They seem radiantly happy. I am glad for his sake he followed her so soon. As you saw from some of the letters I showed you, he felt rather lost without her. Still, it was some comfort for him when I got into touch with her and could tell him about her a bit and convey messages. I owe a lot to that old man. Where, in my young life, should I have been without him? So understanding of my "peculiarities," and never ruffled. He says he is very glad to be rid of his "old bones," and had a wonderfully peaceful passing . . . I'll tell you some more when you get back.

Thursday.

. . . . . . The dear old man turned up again and told me a lot of things too long to relate now. But what do you think? He urged me to have that absurd old diary of mine published—what is left of it. I said, *never*! He said it would do a lot of good and help quite a number of people to realise that clairvoyance isn't all rubbish and charlatanism. He seemed most insistent, and told me some of the spirits on the other side are very keen on the idea. That's all very fine. But, good Lord, my sister would have a fit. Besides, I'm damned if I want to be a sort of Daisy Ashford! No thank you!

Extract from a letter written in 1927.

. . . . . Contacted the E.B. this morning in my meditation. Among other things he said the Brothers are afraid there will have to be another war before very long. (17) Humanity has not learnt its lesson. We are at present living in the Cycle of Mars, the vibrations of which tend to inflame the passions of spiritually unevolved Man. Had Mankind been more advanced, these vibrations would have acted in a much higher way and not resulted in contentiousness and warlike activities. When I wanted to know whether I should live to see this new war when it comes, he said: " My son, we are not fortune-tellers. It is not well that people should see into their own personal future with any degree of accuracy, it would render them too negative." I had never thought of that before, but it is quite true). The E.B. went on to say that only sometimes it is permitted to give certain people a hint about the future (as I myself have done on occasions) where the choice between two given directions is involved. It is sometimes permitted to warn them that such and such a course of action may result in evil to themselves. But whether they will heed the warning is another matter.

He put all this in better language than I have, but that is the gist of what he said . . . . . Old J. says I ought to have an exhibition of my pictures. I said, what on earth for, I don't want to sell them? He even suggested my sending one to the Academy! Never . . . . I have given rather too many treatments to-day and feel reduced to a state of " wet raggishness."

(This is the last letter I received from my husband. Except for a few week-ends, we were never parted again until his death, six years later).

AFTERWORD

It only remains now, for me who has acted as a none too competent annotator to this Diary (see Appendix) to write this brief Afterword, which is more especially addressed to those flexible-minded individuals who are willing to believe that there is more between heaven and earth than has been dreamt of in the philosophy of the materialist.

That the "hero" of these pages (to use a Victorian expression) was a man of integrity who never prostituted his gifts for money or any sordid purpose seems too obvious to comment upon. True, he may have had a few minor faults—who has not?—but these only rendered him the more appealing.

As to the "Elder Brother" who figures so prominently in the script, there seems every reason to believe that he was one of those High Initiates of Arcane Science known to theosophists under the name of Masters, Mahatmas or Great Teachers, and to the Yogis as Maharishis. These great Entities have reached a stage of spiritual evolution far in advance of the "man in the street," and having shed every vestige of selfishness seek only to guide and teach those who possess the necessary aspirations and qualifications, as also indirectly to uplift and influence Mankind in general as far as may be possible. One of the methods the Masters employ for this purpose is to project a powerful thought-form into the *mental space*, so that those who can respond to its vibrations may elaborate it and clothe it in their own particular type of literary expression. Thus to the student of Occultism, it is not ıa matter of surprise to find a number of writers expressing the same thought—writers perhaps living thousands of miles apart from each other, and writing to all intents and purposes on entirely different subjects, or at any rate from an entirely different standpoint. Many of these authors have obviously no conscious knowledge of Occultism at all, and yet they have echoed the substance of what the Masters have been telling their pupils for years.

For example they have pointed out in effect that, although there is lawfulness *within* the nations, there is anarchy *between* the nations. This idea was convincingly elaborated by Prof. Stratton of Harvard University, in his convincing and impressive book *International Delusions*, wherein, just as the Masters have declared, he states that any attempts to govern this world through a system of "lying and cheating and stealing and killing" must inevitably lead to disaster; a pronouncement which has only come too true. Indeed what could be more apt than the E.B.'s phrase: "the multitude of unruly children which constitute humanity"; for it is only children who fight and squabble, whereas sane adults display brotherhood . . . But it would not be in place for me here to discourse upon what I employed as my thesis for *Man is My Theme*,* long before, as far as I was concerned, the publication of this Diary and Letters was ever mooted; I merely mention it as one modest example of how the Masters seek to disseminate their ideas through widely differing channels. Not that my own testimony provides any proof of this: only those who develop the necessary faculties to contact the Masters for themselves can obtain first-hand proofs anent the existence of these exalted Beings and their various activities. Indeed, to those pure souls, like the diarist who was imbued with the spirit of service, They reveal themselves in accordance with the ancient occult maxim, namely, "when the pupil is ready, the Teacher is forthcoming." C.S.

---

*Mostly re-written under the title of *Man, The Unruly Child*. (*The Aquarian Press*, 1953)

APPENDIX

Notes by

CYRIL SCOTT.

(1) That a boy who had the power to see the spirits of the departed should be upset by the idea of death seems illogical. But not more so than the whole Victorian attitude to death, which had obviously made an impression on his subconscious mind. He alludes to this later on in the text.

(2) In this connection *Fairies at Work and Play*, by Geoffry Hodson is well worth reading.

(3) According to Occultism the physical body is interpenetrated with and surrounded by *subtle bodies* perceptible to clairvoyants. The grossest of these is the so-termed *etheric double* or health aura, in which in the case of malignancy a crab-like *elemental*, as it is called, may be seen by those possessing the necessary extension of vision. Although doctors believe that the word cancer was applied to malignant growths because they have tentacles and cling to the surrounding tissues, it is more likely that the name for the disease had a much earlier origin and came into being when the human race was much more clairvoyant than it is in these days of materialism.

(4) The fact that this little nature-spirit was reminiscent of fairy-tale books with their descriptions and drawings is apt to awaken scepticism on the grounds that the boy's vision must have been coloured by his own imagination. Occultists maintain, however, that clairvoyance originally influenced folk-lore and fairy-stories.

241

(5) This finding is borne out by other clairvoyants, in that disease conditions show themselves as dark shadows in the *etheric double* over the seat of the dis-disturbance. By means of Dr. Kilner's Screens it has now become possible to prove this without the aid of clairvoyance.

(6) The idea of a body without a soul is, to an occultist, not as absurd as it may sound on the surface. Leaving aside the materialistic view that there is no such thing as a soul in the sense the Christian accepts the term, the orthodox Christian himself believes that a soul inhabits a body and vacates it at the moment of death. And yet in the case of a certain number of aged people this is not always correct; for the soul has been known to leave the body some years prior to its final dissolution. When this occurs we have what is called "second childhood"; a state which indicates that the body has been left to the so-termed *body elemental*. But to a fuller understanding of this, Occultism requires to be studied. The matter is too long and complex to discourse upon in these Notes.

(7) Whether the boy was seeing what in Indian Occult-ism is called The Akashic Records (The Memory of Nature) or merely seeing the "astral" counterparts of what had once been, I am not in a position to say. In any event his findings are borne out by the experience of a clairvoyante I once knew; though the incident was not concerned with Harlech but with Rome. While she and her party were being shown the sights by a *cicerone*, she astounded him by pointing out that in such and such a place there used to be, say, an archway, a tower, an old door, which she described, and so on. In fact he was so

astonished at her "erudition" that finally he said: "Signora, your knowledge of Roman History is most remarkable." As it so happened, her knowledge of Roman History was absolutely nil!

(8) It looks as if in this instance the boy actually was able to read The Akashic Records. But that does not prove that Mr. Patmore was correct when he said that the priests the lad saw clairvoyantly were Druids. In his enlightening book *The Occult Sciences in Atlantis*, Lewis Spence writes in his chapter headed " The Atlantean Cult in Britain:" . . . when it was found necessary, for ritual purposes, to fix the approximate dates of the seasons of plantation and growth, they (the ancient folk) arranged . . . blocks in the circle in such a manner as to catch the rising gleams of the sun on these important days." He adds: "Stonehenge is assuredly a "temple" built after the manner of that of Poseidon at Cercenes."

(9) While reading about the Druids the boy evidently sensed that they had possessed considerable occult knowledge—a matter which occultists have good reason to believe is correct.

(10) Two seers I have known have corroborated this finding about Nelson. As for the devas in general, the word deva is a Sanscrit word which figures much in Indian Occultism and means literally "shining one". Much about the devas is also to be found in Theosophical literature. There are water devas, air devas, cloud devas, mountain devas, tree devas, etc. There are also devas connected with music, and with halls in which much of the finer types of music are performed. Music devas, known in Indian Occultism as The

243

Gandharvas, have a lot to do with the inspiring of composers. Other devas inspire poets; though much that goes by the name of poetry nowadays is certainly not deva-inspired. The same may be said of much modern music.

(11) In the science of Yoga this energy is called "prana", and is visible to clairvoyant sight. Mesmer believed it to be a fluid. We may presume that 'Miss Ball' possessed a good deal of animal magnetism which she was able to transfer to her patients.

(12) To the sceptic nothing appears such a convincing disproof of Spiritism as the utter triviality of the messages transmitted by some spirits, and the fact that they give themselves out as having been celebrities when on earth. A little more reflection coupled with some occult knowledge, however, would serve to dispel this sceptism unless ingrained in the temperament. The materialist argues that because the messages are so trivial they must perforce be the fraudulent invention of the medium's mind, and therefore no such things as spirits exist. Another theory—a far-fetched one—is that they emanate from the medium's subconscious mind. These contentions are coloured by the curious assumption that if spirits really did exist, by the mere fact of having shed their physical bodies they would have shed most of their characteristics as also their ignorance. Yet why posit the miraculous? Does a man by doffing his overcoat become a changed being, or does a man, merely by changing his environment suddenly and miraculously change himself? Obviously not. Hence if trivial messages come through, the natural assumption would be that they come from trivial-minded entities,

and not that they do not come from any entity as all. As for pretending to be some deceased celebrity, like Shakespeare for instance, just as there is a certain class of people on the earth-plane with a very crude sense of humour, so are there spirits with the same unpleasant attribute. Nor must we forget that vanity often plays a conspicuous part in terrestial life and will not be erradic- in a moment on the so-termed astral plane. As a musician who among other things has composed a number of songs, I am reminded of the many versifiers who have sent me the most nauseating doggerel to set to music, the senders in their vanity believing their verses to be of the highest merit. I am also reminded of a story told to me by one of my publishers, who inform- ed me that a certain composeress submitted a composi- tion every day by post. These compositions savoured very much of Chopin liberally diluted with water! and did not seem of sufficient merit to warrant publication. But when my publisher conveyed this verdict to the worthy lady, he received a vehement reply to the effect that he was a fool, for she was a reincarnation of Chopin, and he little realised what "gems" he was rejecting' . . . . This true story serves to show the power of wishful thinking. Believing in the doctrine of reincarnation and having a great admiration for Chopin but insufficient originality not to compose like Chopin. she imagined in the end that she *was* Chopin; a self-gratifying delusion that will persist into her afterlife unless she faces up to her vanity and takes steps to dissolve it. As to the entity who affirmed she was Sappho, she may have said this in the hope of im-pressing Mr. Patmore so that he should endeavour

245

to get her very platitudinous verses published; she herself believing them to be of great importance.

(13) It is not an entirely uncommon occurrence for a deva of a somewhat low grade to overshadow a person of indifferent talent. Sometimes a deva of this type is anxious to improve mankind by the use of rather naive methods. Thus it happens that people with no special aptitude for literary composition suddenly find themselves with an urge to write scripts of an "improving nature" couched in somewhat biblical language. Though these scripts purport to convey a new Message, they frequently convey little else but "spiritual platitudes" clothed in a slightly new guise.

(14) This incident serves to show how very superior true clairvoyance-plus-clairaudience is to trance-mediumship; that is, unless the trance-medium is of outstanding capacity. What we have to remember is that an entity functioning in its subtle astral body is trying to use the medium's brain in order to express itself. But as her brain may be a very inadequate instrument for the purpose, it is often like, say, a great pianist trying to produce beautiful music out of a very poor piano. The fault does not lie with the musician but with the instrument. Not realising all this, people who visit a trance-medium with a view of getting in touch with their departed relatives or friends, are very often disappointed with the results obtained.

(15) The late Mrs. A. Chaplin, of Crowhurst, Sussex, —a remarkable clairvoyante—made a similar observation about Marseilles when she visited the Riviera between 1920-30. Her findings relative to Monte Carlo were also similar to those mentioned by the diarist in

246

his next letter. She was a pupil of one of "The Elder Brothers," never used her faculties in a professional capacity, and was a woman of the highest integrity.

(16) This would seem to be a reference to Dr. Carl Wickland, who subsequently wrote that enlightening book, *Thirty Years Among The Dead*. Having discovered that many people suffering from strange mental states and even from physical symptoms were obsessed by spirits of the departed, he contrived to dislodge the obsessing entities by means of electricity. Sometimes, however, he was able to persuade them to withdraw merely by talking to them. His wife who had pronounced mediumistic powers aided him in his work. The book repays study, and should open the eyes of people who regard possession by "evil spirits" as either a fanciful superstition or else an impossibility in our "enlightened age." According to the New Testament narrative, Jesus of Nazareth had the power to exorcise such "evil spirits"; but it would seem that the attitude of the Protestant Church regarding this is on a par with its attitude to Spiritualism in general., *viz.* either antagonistic, sceptical, or at best, hazy.

(17) This quite accords with messages received from the Initiates by psychics of my own acquaintance about fifteen years before the second great war eventuated. And yet, strange to say, and pleasing to sceptics, when war was imminent, the spiritualists declared that it would never happen. Why this terrible "bloomer"? My own opinion is that either wishful thinking on the part of mediums prevented them from getting the messages through uncoloured, or else that the astral plane spirits

were confident that they could avert the war even at the last minute. All of which tends to increase my respect for the diarist whose attitude towards the denizens of the other planes was entirely reasonable. In fact, knowing them as he did, he never regarded them as infallible but with the same capacity to err as human beings who are still on earth.